Alyson Rudd was born in Liverpool, where she grew up in a Shankly-dominated world. She was educated at the London School of Economics, before moving on to financial journalism. In 1992 she began to write about football, and is now a football writer and columnist for *The Times*.

She lives in Barnes, south-west London, with her husband, one son and a growing collection of old football boots.

ALSO BY ALYSON RUDD

Matthew Harding – Pursuing the Dream

astroturf blonde

ALYSON RUDD

HEADLINE

First published in 1998
by HEADLINE BOOK PUBLISHING

First published in paperback in 1999
by HEADLINE BOOK PUBLISHING

10 9 8 7 6 5 4 3 2 1

ISBN 0 7472 6093 1

Printed and bound in Great Britain by
Mackays of Chatham plc, Chatham, Kent

HEADLINE BOOK PUBLISHING
A division of Hodder Headline PLC
338 Euston Road
London NW1 3BH

CONTENTS

v

ACKNOWLEDGEMENTS

I would like to thank my parents for humouring me, the boys in the park for suffering me and Adrian for encouraging me.

CHAPTER ONE

'hey! that's a woman'

I was all alone in the draughty and cramped ladies toilet, hurriedly pulling on a pair of shorts. The grey pipes creaked and a tap dripped into a cracked sink, but I could hear the rest of my team talking and laughing. They were packed into one of the small changing rooms and preparing for a game that would be much like any of the other football matches that take place on the Astroturf pitches of Caledonian Park, North London. Except perhaps for the fact that 21 of the participants would be men and one would be a woman.

I knew only two of the men in my team reasonably well, and a couple more by sight, but I could not find them and walked out awkwardly, a slight distance off to one side, as both teams made their way to the pitch. There were a couple of raised eyebrows when several of my team acknowledged that I was wearing the same strip as they were. Clearly they had not been told that a girl was involved, and I was glad. It was of no more significance than the fact that a chemical engineer had also been asked along to make up the numbers. But I was relieved when Greg arrived, late, as usual, and made a few formal introductions.

'What position do you usually play then?' asked the captain.

For some reason, I felt obliged to launch into a potted resumé of my gifts and my flaws.

'I don't take players on and I have only ever played in defence once. The best thing I do is release a defence-splitting pass so I think I'd be better off playing in the hole behind two strikers or as an off-striker . . .'

But he was not listening. He was struggling to stay on his feet as he sniggered and snorted at the delightful double entendre of 'in the hole'.

'She plays, get this, in the hole. Hey, Joey mate, guess where she plays?'

Oh dear. No one had tittered when Terry Venables had spoken of playing a striker in the hole, or John Motson had reported on the fact. It did not bode well. And this was supposed to be a dream come true.

What does it feel like when a dream comes true?

The phone had rung as I sat in my study. It was Greg, a chap I used to work with, who tends to open a conversation sounding as if you were both already half way through it. So he laughed. 'Ha, ha, Ally, how are you? Greg here.' I was busy and probably brusque so Greg went straight to the point. He was short of players for a match the following Wednesday. He was not trying to make a dream come true, he simply knows a good many people who are always keen for a game and I am on that list. But I had not been asked before, at least not in a 'just another player' sort of way. Greg had asked me along to games because I was a woman and there are tournaments that insist on one member of the squad being female but never had he asked me just because I play football.

And that was the dream. The fantasy was to be ordinary. I had secretly seethed as male friends or colleagues had pushed their battered sports bag or Tesco carrier under their desk muttering about being asked to play football at short notice. No one was going to ask me in spite of the fact that every time anyone I have ever met mentions they are part of a work or Sunday team I always say: 'And if you are ever desperate, just give me a call.' Over the years I had improved to the point where my presence would be better than the team being a player short, but all my football alongside men had been organised by me. I was in a similar position to somebody who is very wealthy and organises giant parties with extravagant entertainment in order to find a constant stream of friends. Organising football games does not cost anything but involves time and effort not everyone can afford. So if I arranged the match, I could play in it. It is not the same as being begged to take part and it did not really bother me, but now and again I dreamed of it being someone else who had to make the phone calls and arrange the pitch – but I still got to join in.

Was this happening now?

'So you really need me to play, I'm not just there as back-up in case of emergency?' Greg assured me he was indeed desperate and had thought of me because I told him to in such circumstances, and, anyway, the pitch was fairly close to where I lived and the reason he was short of players was because the venue involved too long a journey for some of his regulars.

The match was a contest between his office and his Sunday league team. I was needed to represent his office. It sounded quite sweet. I knew Greg's Sunday team took the game seriously and pitied him the hours of cajoling he must have put in to convince his overweight and unfit work colleagues to face them. It was a foolish conclusion for me to have drawn. There were a few plump bottoms and beer bellies around but no lack of feverish desire and will to win.

My team acceded to my request to play behind a sprightly and very young centre forward. It transpired that I really was needed; neither side had any substitutes – and if they had, they would in any case no doubt have refused to sit part of the game out while a woman was in the starting line-up. Our diminutive striker had been picked up a few minutes earlier from a small group of youngsters who were loitering and hoping to find a game and dreaming in their own way of putting their age behind them, of being discovered, of being hailed a hero. I was worried for a moment that another of these hopefuls would be allowed to take my place. It would have been insulting and unfair and perhaps that was the only reason it did not happen. There was little evidence that anyone was interested in whether I could play or not. I had turned up and that was that.

And so the game began. Some kids watched and pointed in my direction. 'Hey, that's a woman!' I pounced on a loose ball and immediately heard my captain scream 'pass it, pass it' as though I was the village idiot and might be tempted to pick the ball up off the floor and run off to the showers with it singing 'catch me if you can'. And so, shaken by my captain's hysteria, I panicked and just hacked aimlessly at the ball. It zipped along the fake grass and was easily mopped up by a defender. I knew immediately that was it. That fleeting moment had been my audition. Casting directors need two seconds of dialogue or song to know if you fit the bill, or rather to decide that you do not fit it, and my team immediately decided I was hopelessly miscast.

I could hear their thoughts. She can't play, what's going on? And so the remaining 43 minutes of the first half were hell. Greg was playing for his Sunday team and no one on my side had the courage of faith to pass to me. I scurried about and tried to look as if I belonged but it takes a level of courage far in excess of anything I possessed to keep on calling for the ball when it never arrives.

Normally, I would have been past help. If a game goes badly my confidence slips away and my shoulders droop. But I was more angry with my team than with myself. I had not had a chance bar that early touch to embarrass myself. Out of frustration and a sense of injustice I could feel optimism and determination returning.

There was a switch at half-time. Andy, Greg's brother, who had played alongside me in Regent's Park and knew what I could and could not do, had been our goalkeeper but was now put in midfield. And joy of joys, he passed the ball to me, ran for the return and I passed it back. It was a neat one-two, nothing more, but for me it was a shimmering breakthrough. I will not pretend I won the game for us single-handed but I became part of the performance. Having seen that giving the ball to me was not to be branded a reckless fool, my team-mates forgot their prejudices. I 'nutmegged' an embarrassed opponent, whose own captain bawled in disgust, and then skipped past him to receive the ball again. It is much, much, easier to play well when you feel you are walking on air, when you are too preoccupied with the actual game to feel niggled by side issues.

My timing was magical. I held on to the ball while a

defender flung himself in my direction and let it go just as he committed himself. Most of what I did was unremarkable and probably the least you should be expected to do if you agree to be part of a fairly serious contest and it was a pleasure in itself just to be competent. But what I could hardly have imagined would happen, happened. I started trying my little Matthew Le Tissier impressions, something I only ever do when I am at my most uninhibited. Remarkably they came off. A high and powerful cleared ball thundered in my direction and I trapped it with the side of my heel and flicked it into Andy's path.

Afterwards, as I approached the changing room, I heard my captain saying what a marvellous piece of skill that had been. Greg agreed with him and caught my eye. He had seen me try that before and fail but the important point was that it was intentional, not that I would be able to repeat it every time.

I did not score the winning goal or any goal. To be honest I did not even come close. When a game with men begins the goalposts appear the same size and shape as any other but once the match is underway they shrink and are surrounded by a force-field. I am rarely disparaging of a goal-less draw in the Premiership because I know the route to goal is strewn with pitfalls and the sort of obstacles used in fables about princes who get to marry the princess only if they bring back three golden apples guarded by two-headed bears, fire-breathing dragons and a pack of wolves who have not eaten for 100 years. And then the king says: 'Nah, I've changed my mind.'

Having received the ball at the edge of the penalty area, there is an in-built desire to run towards the goal or unleash a beautiful shot but, against men, this is impossible. They ran towards me in the text-book style known as 'closing a forward down' but it felt as though they were starving me of oxygen, not just space. I tried to shoot, just once, but I doubt anyone considered it a shot. As the ball travelled through the air the goalmouth drifted out of focus and I, too, wondered what it was I had tried to pull off.

At set pieces it was no easier. In the park, in friendlier, less frenzied games, I have developed a technique of loitering at the far post ready to volley beyond the goalkeeper. I have scored with the most aesthetically pleasing volley ever seen in park football. On tough, testosterone Astroturf, however, I was not given time to draw my foot back, let alone make contact. Heading was out of the question too. What was the point in trying when any of these blokes would rather their left eye popped out of its socket than be responsible for a failure to clear the ball from the forehead of a girlie.

Even so I left the ground trying hard not to smirk. I had not made a single error in that second half, I had heard the opposition's captain call for me to be marked tighter and my own captain mutter 'well played'. I had been nervous, towards the end, of putting in a cross with my left foot, but by then such a display of weakness could be forgiven and someone ran over to give me an alternative outlet and even praised me for holding the ball up for him. Could a woman legitimately be part of a more competitive match, a professional match, I wondered, as I drove home? There is not much difference between having a slightly built Eastern European player whose English is extremely poor for a team-mate and having a woman. The woman would miss out on the dressing-room camaraderie but then so would a man who could not communicate in the same language. There might be tension if the woman dated one of the players or was suspected of flirting, but is there any less tension if a player has an affair with another's wife?

One day a woman will appear who is fast and strong and can make a ball spin into whichever part of the back of the net that she chooses. She will be so talented that to exclude her will break equal opportunities law, and the European Court of Human Rights will insist that she be given a chance to prove herself at the highest level. There will only ever be one woman like this but the fear that there will be more will tear at men's hearts and egos. She will be the biggest star in the game's history, she will be rich, she will be loved to her face and hated behind it. International goalkeepers will shoot themselves for failing to save her sweetly struck shot from 35 yards out that wins her team the Champions League and then the Super Cup. Her colleagues' girlfriends will storm out of the stadium when the men embrace her at the final whistle. Football-mad geneticists will wonder which player should fertilise her eggs to create the greatest footballer that ever lived. She will retire at the peak of her fame and successfully manage a lower league side, taking it far enough to rub shoulders with and rile Manchester United, while just occasionally coming on as a sub to score the winner if necessary. That woman will not be me. But I doubt her joy will be any more intense than the happiness I feel when I am just about acceptable on the Astroturf.

If I had grown up in a world where women's teams are accepted I might not have summoned such resolve to prove myself among men. Today a three-year-old girl can play with her Barbie doll, having first dressed her in Barbie's official football strip. It comprises a purple and white striped shirt with a red collar and red shorts. The football boots are dainty and white, but then so are Paolo Di Canio's. Barbie used to be 30 years behind the times. If I had believed in Barbie's world when I was three I would have grown up thinking pink is beautiful, that perky, large breasts were standard, and a diamanté encrusted ball-gown with glass slippers represented the ultimate dream. Today's toddler thinks a football strip is as essential an item as Barbie's beach barbecue set. Surely the manufacturers are suddenly 30 years ahead of the trend.

I have just finished explaining to a TV researcher why I cannot attend a studio discussion programme that needs me to say women's football is as entertaining as men's and they should be paid to play it. All discussions on women and football are off-beam because they compare the women's leagues to the Premiership. The valid comparison is with male amateur soccer, with those Sunday morning leagues where dads with bald patches mix with students and an almighty row is erupting because the goals have no nets on them. This is the highest rung of men's football that I have participated in and there is room for women in it – only most such teams are affiliated to the Football Association and their rules insist on segregation.

One London league, however, is not affiliated. Its various members have their own reasons for wanting to be run separately but the Homerton Academicals had among its objections the fact that women could not play in their team. Only, no women actually play in their team. During one beer-infused afternoon this paradox was mulled over and Greg, for Greg has a finger in many football pies, suggested they ask me to play, to prove their point. Naturally, I was as excited as Barbie and Ken on a first date – to be a walking, talking, kicking principle is, obviously, a great honour.

It was agreed that, since they had two substitutes, I

would play for only 25 minutes. 'That's fine,' I thought, 'if I play really well, I'll get longer.' And I trawled through my wishful back catalogue of 30-yard drives and 50-yard unstoppable runs – an act that precedes every match I ever play in. I knew one of the other subs and he gave me a lift. I babbled. I babbled about how we must not be late, about whether I would actually play after all. I was nervous of letting them all down and at the same time of not being wanted.

In the event I was treated with almost comical courtesy. The captain swore viciously at latecomers and turned and smiled sweetly at me before launching a barrage of abuse at a full back who had lost his car keys. But these verbal attacks were necessary. Without them even some of the regulars would have failed to take the match seriously enough. At this level, organisation and discipline can win you the game.

As I have a tendency to view all my poor performances as unutterably appalling and all my reasonable ones as shout-it-from-the-hill-top-I-am-a-star, it is devilishly difficult for me to construct a totally accurate assessment of my contribution. But on balance, I think I was passable. Certainly I passed for a bloke. To my sheer and unadulterated delight I overheard a member of the other team call out that they were not marking that bloke with the pony tail closely enough. And I was the only player with a pony tail. Quite possibly some women would have found this insulting or demeaning or depressing. But in a sports bra and a baggy football shirt I do not have any obvious bosom and that does not bother me – after all there are under-wired bras for those clingy lycra tops, and the chap who had mentioned me had not been closer than 30 yards so there was no inadvertent slur on my face, no need to rush to a clinic for electrolysis to remove an unsightly moustache. His team-mate put him straight anyway.

'OK, but it's not a bloke. It's a girl.'

'Really?'

'Apparently. That's what their keeper told me anyway.'

All right, at this point perhaps I ought to have wondered just how unattractive I looked, but I didn't. To be mistaken for a man in this context was a massive compliment. It meant I could blend in, be part of a team that I would have once thought to be beyond my limits. I tried one shot which required a half-decent save and I laid the ball off for the captain to strike a much better effort and received warm praise all round. There was, though, a collective silent sigh of relief when I went off. They had done their bit and I had done mine. The principle had triumphed. I had not been maimed or lost my ability to carry a child and the game had not degenerated into a sexual orgy or a gang rape. Two fingers to the FA, then.

CHAPTER TWO

heroes and buddies

It was beyond dusk. The gloom was far-reaching for there
were few houses or street lamps nearby and the floodlights
had yet to warm up. The Astroturf pitch was peeling at the
edges and surrounded on three sides by a high bank, thick
bush and patchy railings. The changing rooms were locked,
deserted and, oddly, graffiti-free. It was early spring but this
was a season-anonymity zone. I peered in vain for a sign of
the opposition – just one of their players would have done
to keep our hopes up. There was little chit-chat among the
gang. To speak was to announce for every sound had a
sharp clarity in this vacuum. No cars, no distant laughter,
no dogs barking. The sound of sports bags being unzipped
interrupted the soulless breeze. I began to wonder if my
credibility as player-manager/fixture-arranger was on the
wane. I had absolutely no idea who the opposition were.

It began with a phone call at work.

'Can I speak to Ally?'

This immediately sent me into footie mode; I am not
called Ally by anyone other than my soccer chums. The
chap on the phone was called Terry. He had heard that
I had a team keen for the odd 11-a-side game and his lads
needed some practice and had a spare two-hour slot booked

on a full-size pitch. I emphasised that we were used to very, very friendly six-a-side games, usually between ourselves, and that we played for enjoyment of the game and not as an excuse to kick, elbow and find our inner lout.

'Oh yeah, that sounds like us,' said Terry. So we agreed to the contest. Terry had not been curious as to why he was dealing with a woman. He did not even ask if I would be playing or if any other women would be involved. Right on, I thought.

But now, stranded in the wastelands of south-east London, I wondered if that conversation had been about football at all. Maybe 'practice' was a euphemism for 'crack'. Perhaps by speaking of enjoyment I had unwittingly been eulogising about the use of recreational drugs. I did not know who Terry was, other than he worked in a paper factory. I remembered that when he told me who had told him about me, I had no clue who he was speaking of and had simply beamed at the realisation that my footballing connections were so myriad I could not possibly be expected to keep track of them all.

Then, out of the darkness, strolled an ominous looking man. He was a short, slightly built young fellow but he had an iron bar slung nonchalantly over his shoulder. It was the caretaker and his arrival sparked the big event into life. There was light and there was another team. I would say, man for man and one woman they were two years younger and two stone heavier on average and at least 60 times meaner with their glances over the opposition. Sometimes a game is lost before a ball is kicked and this was one of those occasions. Still, I was the manager, I had to organise the team, maintain morale.

'I'm sorry, I'm sorry, they look a bit tough don't they?'

'Don't worry Ally, our skill and tactical acumen will shake them.'

We lost 13–2. Or maybe it was 12–2. There was no disputed goal, we simply stopped counting. It was a shame because we had all been so looking forward to giving our superior understanding of the game a real run-out on a full-size pitch. However, unless you are exceptionally gifted, cerebral application counts for nothing when you face muscle. This happens all the time in non-League football and sometimes in the professional game too. I have seen Bury play twice, when they were in the Second Division, and on both occasions they won because they were bigger than their opponents.

We, too, were bulldozed. I played for the first and last time in my life at right full back. This meant I was constantly trying to dispossess a man who comes in at number one as the most annoying person I have ever played against. He was fat, fat in that comic book style of fatness with the fat sitting Tweedle-Dum style around his waist. He would receive the ball and waddle towards me. I would attempt to poke the ball from under his feet but I could not reach it. I bounced off his stomach before I was within two yards of the ball. And he would keep possession by slowly turning complete circles. Like fools we fell into the trap. I could not get the ball so eventually one of my team-mates would dash over to help and so, having created space for a midfield colleague, Tweedle would then play the ball out to him. Had we been more interested in damage limitation we would have called his bluff and allowed the clock to tick away to reduce the amount of time they had available to score. But almost to the end we thought we could salvage something.

The referee for this debacle was the real thing. Sometimes such games are refereed and sometimes they are not but it is rare for a friendly, ad hoc match to be overseen by a man in full refereeing gear, with full refereeing attitude. His presence offered us a glimmer of hope for he was 'a gentleman'.

'No, no, no, you can't shove a lady like that,' he would say, having blown his whistle for a foul which comprised the brush of arm hair against arm hair.

'I didn't fucking touch her, ref,' was the inevitable response.

The opposition were riled and I should have switched from defence to centre forward and fallen over inside the penalty area a couple of dozen times to force an unlikely victory. But, if I had, there would have been an incident and possibly a very serious incident that might have made the papers and generated a national debate about a woman's right to play football with men. I did not want an incident, I wanted to be treated the same as everyone else and so our only hope of salvation was swept off on the Southwark wind as I kept an increasingly low and dispirited profile.

And that is one of the amazing things about football. I was disappointed, downcast and a little embarrassed but I had a brilliant time and could not wait until I played again. If football has your soul, you do not forsake it just because you lost (maybe it was 14–1), you count your blessings that you were fit to play and were part of a team in the first place.

I played in my first match when I was 18 and played perfectly well, I seem to remember, until, ten minutes into the game, I sprained my ankle. It was an awkward sprain and took an age to shake off. Then I played in my second match in rare inner London snow and sprained the same ankle after two minutes. By the time I was fit again the group of Italians who organised the five-a-side had left my college. The London School of Economics had a reputation for sporting un-excellence. It had no facilities whatsoever. There was a rugby team but it had to travel 120 miles to its home fixtures. With hindsight the Italians who had praised my skill and judgement were either being incredibly nice or flirting. Only now, 16 years on, can compliments be considered close to justifiable.

One of my mum's favourite phrases is: 'Ooooh, she's got little footballer's legs.' She would say this when I was two, and again to my acute mortification when I was 14 and again to my immense pride when I was 30. She was and is right. I am blonde but not leggy, I was skinny but had stocky legs. I dreamed more about playing for Liverpool than I did about being a famous actress or a beauty queen – which was just as well considering my legs are shorter than my body.

The reason I found myself humbled one day on a wind-swept Astroturf pitch has its beginnings in those dreams. I suppose every young girl is gripped with a passion or obsession and it is usually pop, pony or popcorn orientated. For me it was football. Or more specifically Liverpool and most non-British European national teams. I even know the precise moment football became for me a wondrous world of soaring emotions and escapism. I was eight years old and had been in the garden and wandered in to see my dad watching a match on TV. I watched too, and noticed the way one player had run along the touchline evading tackle after tackle by skipping or altering his pace and pushing the ball ahead of the challenge. I clearly remember thinking this must be a hugely talented player because I had not noticed anyone do that before. I thought it was, quite simply, beautiful. I asked my dad who it was and, in a voice feigning surprise that I did not know, he answered that it was Steve Heighway.

That sealed my devotion to Liverpool. Until then I had been a Liverpool fan in the same way as I was a Lancashire cricket fan and Wigan rugby league fan. They were the right answers, but I did not know why they were the right answers for me. I was born in Liverpool and brought up on its very outskirts. My granddad was an Everton supporter and as a rule I spoke up for the opposite of whatever he believed in because it was a good laugh watching him splutter his indignation.

But I did learn from him how serious this partisanship business can be. He was prepared to accept that Everton might have performed below par but never that the opposition were superior. Once, when I looked through his Everton season ticket book, granddad held his breath, torn between love of granddaughter and love of club. In the end he was saved by my mum who realised that, if I were to rip just one ticket, a family feud would ensue. She told me not to touch it again. As a result of that ticking off I grew up believing that granddad was a senior figure at Goodison Park and that the stubs and tickets I had held in my hand must have been valuable share certificates. There was always a packet of Everton mints in the top drawer of his bureau and for some reason this confirmed my suspicion that Everton's fortunes were linked to granddad's personal liquidity.

Meanwhile I doodled LFC in the corner of my homework and developed a major crush on Mr Heighway. This was a highly honourable crush for my devotion was based on his ability as opposed to his movie star looks. He did not have movie star looks, he did not need them because – and here was the *coup de grace* – Steve Heighway was a university graduate. Much as I adored his team-mates, Heighway stood apart. He was intelligent, loyal and under-rated. He was the architect of every Liverpool victory and it burned my heart to see the players rush to hug Kevin Keegan after he had pounced on a cross from Heighway to score. At such moments Heighway would quietly applaud the goal, but rarely did he career over to Keegan to join in the mass embrace.

It was this sense of detachment that made him heroic and so it came to pass that one glorious summer's day my parents appeared early at the junior school gates and said it was time for my dental appointment. They winked. There was no dental appointment. They were off to the beach in Formby and had decided, not unreasonably, that I would want to visit a sports shop in the vicinity that was owned by Heighway. The numbness followed by faint nausea then panic is what I imagine Lottery hopefuls feel when they need just one more number. My palpitations increased with every mile we covered. Dad parked right outside the shop and I did not think my heart would ever start up again. It was still and hot and the street was silent.

'Well here we are.'

Silence.

'Are you going in then?'

'I can't.'

'Don't be silly.'

'I can't. He might be in there, he might see me.'

More to the point he might have seen me and the neon lights flashing on my forehead proclaiming my ridiculous infatuation. I knew perfectly well that had he looked me in the eye every single detail of my devotion would be all too obvious and he, and I, would be embarrassed. And it was more complex than that. I was nine, nearly ten and hopeful that when I was 16 I would be an attractive and intelligent woman whose views on football would be interesting and informative. That was when I wanted to meet Mr Heighway.

I did not go in the shop. But it was an important day. I was such a big Liverpool fan that my parents had deceived my school. It conferred a status of sorts and I never looked back. I was allowed to eat my tea in front of the telly if there was football on while the rest of the family sat at the table in the dining room.

'Why can't I sit in the lounge?' I could hear my younger sister wail.

'Shh, it's special, it's football for Alyson.'

I thought I was the only person in England who truly appreciated the level of football played during the World Cup and I was annoyed that my country's efforts were so graceless by comparison. I was allowed to change channels from a big movie to *The Big Match*. I was not chided for sobbing as I sat in the kitchen listening to Radio City's live cup commentary tell me that Liverpool were a goal down. I was forgiven the moods that followed defeat. Perhaps my parents just counted their blessings that I was not a Tranmere Rovers supporter. Perhaps they were glad I was not a boy likely to abandon study in favour of soccer school. Perhaps I was deadly dull and they were grateful I had developed a hobby. Whatever the reason I was fortunate not to be discouraged.

The extremes of emotion have slowly evaporated but the bond with the club has not. If someone, anyone, a complete and utter stranger, is a Liverpool supporter I automatically feel I can trust them, that I already know them. I once travelled from London to Liverpool by train on a Wednesday evening. It was to attend a fourth round FA Cup tie against Bristol Rovers and not really the glamour game worth sneaking off work early for to arrive back in London past 2 a.m. But Keith was emigrating.

Now I hardly knew Keith. I had bumped into him on the stairs at work a few times and had a 'I hear you are a Liverpool fan' type of conversation with him, and then invited him to join a group of us off to Highbury or White Hart Lane. But beyond that I knew nothing about him. However, he let slip he had never been to Anfield. He was a southerner, a 'what happens north of Watford?' sort of southerner and the sort I do not much like, but he was, when all was said and done, a Liverpool supporter and it was wrong for him to leave the country without seeing Anfield.

Of course that was for him to decide. Well, no it wasn't. He was a laid-back lad who needed prompting into action. He had doleful eyes that lit up when I said he could tag along to a match. It was up to me to get him to Anfield. The plan was that as Keith was in the Midlands on sales rep duty, I would travel by train and meet him and two of my Liverpool-supporting friends, who had driven up earlier in the day, at Lime Street station.

My train broke down about five miles from Liverpool. As I checked my watch over and over again I realised the plan had fallen apart. The gang would have left Lime Street to make kick-off. They knew it would be what I would want them to do, I thought bravely. Then I overheard a passenger in the buffet car talking to the steward about the match. I collared him.

'Are you going to the game? Right. We'll share a cab. As soon as the train starts we'll move to the front and we must run to the taxi rank.'

The man looked bemused but agreed. It was only when we slumped into our seats in the taxi that I realised he was a Rovers supporter. For a split second I felt vulnerable. What was I doing taking charge of an older, strange, slightly overweight, well-spoken bloke in a deserted city. But he was already in the process of explaining that although born in Bristol, he had always had the highest regard for Liverpool and to draw the Reds in the Cup represented a Perfect Football Experience. I relaxed. He knew a lot about both teams. We even exchanged business cards and then he ran to the away end and I slid through the last open turnstile on the Kop.

It is strange arriving at a match after it has begun. The communion between players and fans, which is set up after the teams have run out onto the pitch and involves players acknowledging their name being sung, has passed and the unity has fractured as the fans wait for their faith to be restored.

'Bloody awful ball. My bloody grandmother can pass better than that and, bloody hell, she's dead.'

The relationship is usually revived well before the final whistle but without the benefit of the first stage of the ritual, the criticism seemed, to me, to be unfair. And the match and the crowd had found a rhythm that I could not quite enter into until after half-time. I shuffled around the terrace, infiltrating one clutch of supporters after another, listening to their commentary, using strangers as posts to lean on when the crowd surged forward and to hoist myself up on when a goal looked imminent. No matter that ground safety has been improved by scrapping the terraces, to watch a game while standing, particularly among such a vast group, is a special experience. The game, the teams, the action all look so much more immediate, more urgent, more personal. It was there for the fans. You stood, they stood. You tired because they were awful, you forgot you were tired because they were superb.

Amazingly, I even found my friends on the Kop and I travelled back to London in Keith's car. He tried to smoke so I threw his cigarette out of the window and when we stopped for petrol I hid his packet of Benson & Hedges. When his mates at work asked if he enjoyed his first trip to Anfield, he droned on about not being allowed to smoke. I was not invited to his leaving party.

Then a week later Mr Bristol Rovers phoned to say he was in the neighbourhood, should we meet for a lunch-time drink? He sat in my office while I finished off some work and, as we left, I caught a colleague pursing her lips and shaking her head in a 'I wouldn't if I were you' sort of way. How narrow-minded I thought until we sat down with our beer and he unbuttoned his rain coat and started talking about what a 'cute bunny' I was. Fortunately I have met many more people through a love of Liverpool who have turned out to be buddies for a lifetime and we have danced and chanted and moped and snarled over the Reds together.

Club support is an emotional pact that has such an influence over your formative years that, although I have not actually cried over a Liverpool performance for at least three years, I could never cease to care about them. And what else, in childhood and adolescence at least, can provide a package of such deep hurt and intense joy? Appreciation of the artistry of football came first and then the sense of belonging.

We stood as a family near the centre of Liverpool waiting for the bus that carried the team and the FA Cup. I was bemused by the carnival atmosphere. Everyone was holding something red. I held a windmill stick and felt self-conscious.

'Why are there so many people here?'

'Because Liverpool won the Cup.'

I knew that, but the concept of a victory party was new to me. Faces were flushed, there were young children, middle-aged men, old ladies and they all seemed drunk. There were foil and cardboard replicas of the FA Cup displayed in bedroom windows, car aerials had red and white ribbons tied to them, little babies had red and white bobble hats falling over their eyes. I thought it was daft and I did not like being jostled. And then the bus came into view. The roar was delicious. It was serious. Suddenly the haphazard jollity became tribal and organised. Within the same split-second I realised the players, the actual players were moving closer and closer to me, the chant of 'Keegan two, Heighway one, Liverpool three and Newcastle none' started. It replayed in my head for the rest of the summer. My first chant. My first experience of the football crowd as a single, united entity. It was time to go to Anfield.

Well, I could go when I was a bit older. Far from causing me to be distraught, this response only served to heighten the belief that a big live match was an important and

complicated event. And when I was considered old enough
the anticipation, the build-up, watching *Grandstand* before
we left, spotting cars with other fans inside, having a cup
of tea with an aunt who rather fortuitously lived on Anfield
Road and could provide us with parking space and a lecture
(her son supported Everton) was all too much. Dad had not,
I am sure, been to a match since he was married – he never
took football that seriously and is of a generation many of
whom did not maintain so-called bachelor pursuits after
starting a family. I met a football writer on a train once who
was nearer in age to my dad than me and in the course of the
conversation I asked him why his first marriage had failed.
I cannot believe no one had ever asked him this before but
an expression of sudden realisation spread across his face
as he recalled how his beloved Sunderland had reached
Wembley to face Leeds United in the 1973 FA Cup final. It
was Sunderland's finest hour and this man's new wife said
he could not watch the game on TV, he had to go Saturday
shopping with her.

'That's when I realised we were not really suited.'

I cannot remember if he said he saw Sunderland's victory
that day or not and the fact that I can't implies that he didn't.
It is just too awful a concept to take in. Cup final day in our
family was and is always given status, but most of the time
for football I was on my own. It was my private universe
and I was humoured. If I could not persuade dad to give up
an afternoon or evening for a trip to a match then would-be
suitors were allowed a date. Fluff-chinned, gangly teenagers
who would not normally make a girl's heart flutter were
suddenly my best friends if their dad or uncle had a spare
season ticket. They were hopeful at first, but in the end it
killed their ardour. That nearly pretty girl down the road

was apparently transformed into an uncouth tomboy who unsettlingly knew more, or thought she did, about football than her companion, a companion who had been looking forward to teaching his first girlfriend about offside and which were the best and worst players.

Once I had to be carried out through the men's toilets after passing out on the terraces. It brought me round. It is quite a shock to a fifteen-year-old girl's system to witness a giant, stenching urinal. For some reason I thought it was important not to let on how disgusted I was. Of course in the 1970s there were fewer girls at matches, something that did not bother me at all and I would not even have noticed it but for the 'sponge effect'. Men can be quite besotted with their team. They will hug their mates or indeed, any bloke near enough if the occasion warrants it. But put a female close by and their expression of true love for the boys in Red means they cannot resist a kiss. My dad did not like this, and who could blame him, but as long as I knew it was not gratuitous I did not mind. And some men feel they have to project their emotions onto the fairer sex.

'I bet you're worried eh?' if we are a goal behind. 'I bet you're relieved now, eh?' if we equalise. It is as if they need you to cry or scream because they do not feel they can go that far. The only game from that time that I really remember in Technicolor, big-screen, vivid detail was played in September 1978. It is my favourite match of all time and it contained my favourite goal. Football does not come any more perfect than excitedly insisting you have to wear your red and white scarf even if it is a boiling hot afternoon because you have just seen the BBC talk up your team's opponents. Indignant, as well as warm, you dwell on the footage of Ossie Ardiles and

Ricky Villa and the assessment that Spurs' Argentinians will tear Liverpool apart and wonder that anyone can take southern softies seriously.

Then in deep golden sunshine which makes the red paintwork of the stadium shimmer proudly you stand next to your dad, and watch your team win by seven goals to nil. Everyone there that day knew they were part of something almost supernatural. Far from taking the match less seriously as the goals rained in, the Liverpool fans grew ever more expectant. And their team did not disappoint.

The final goal of the rout was the most splendid, the most cruel, the most gorgeous, the most ingenious as Liverpool patronisingly gave Tottenham Hotspur a few seconds of attacking play inside their penalty area and then swept the ball from one side of the pitch to the other as though the zigzags were part of an illustration, not real-time football. Kennedy to Dalglish to Johnson to Heighway who trapped the ball while in mid-air and only a couple of feet from me, to . . . Seemingly no one.

What was Heighway doing? His cross curled high and then drifted like a feather to the far edge of the area but, while it did so, McDermott was running up the centre of the pitch. As the ball fell, McDermott appeared among a battered confusion of white shirts and headed it into the back of the net. The men around me laughed and cheered hysterically. The teams must watch *Grandstand*, too, I thought, as the Spurs players' body language collapsed and the Liverpool players went briefly delirious. It was seamless, pure, instinctive. Once again Heighway kept his celebration to himself but Alan Kennedy, who had touchingly reacted to each goal as if it were a vital equaliser, ran over to my hero and lifted him off the ground in a bear hug. Again Heighway was right in front of me and I averted my gaze as his shorts were pulled upwards in case I caught a glimpse of his underpants.

CHAPTER THREE

the debut

I did try to play back then. My best friend Julie had an older brother who we found one day kicking a ball about with his mate.

'Can we play?'

'No, go away.'

But perhaps because of my crestfallen, 'I have no brother of my own' expression David relented. 'You can play in goal.' Julie thought this was demeaning and she sulkily waved her arms about. But I took wholeheartedly to this unexpected piece of good fortune and dived and jumped and uncomplainingly took the whacks in the stomach and on the nose.

'See, Julie,' said David. 'Alyson is doing this properly. Well done, Alyson.'

I bulged with pride and toyed for the next few months with the notion that I could infiltrate the Liverpool ranks as a goalkeeper. It wore off. Even a naïve nine-year-old knows that goalkeepers are sad, friendless freaks forced to stand apart and dress differently because they have smelly feet and seeping spots. Real goalkeepers were wonderful, of course, but still strange and not to be stood next to at the bus stop.

What was a girl to do? I embarked on secondary education but my grammar school had a bizarre attitude dedicated
to preserving the division of the sexes as it was, and there was
no football on the curriculum for the boys anyway. Girls
were not allowed to wear patent leather shoes in case the
nasty, lascivious boys saw the reflection of their underwear,
so asking for a mixed game of football was fairly pointless. Hockey was reasonable preparation for the mud and
aggression of football, and netball proved useful in terms
of spatial awareness, but they were poor substitutes for the
real thing. Athletics was less frustrating and, although by
the time I started playing football regularly I had lost a lot
of my teenage speed, the belief that I could run was an asset.
As A-Levels loomed football faded into the background. A
Marxist musician boyfriend, who was prepared to humour
my thesis on why The Rutles were far superior to The
Beatles, could not tolerate the fact I wanted to listen to
Sports Report. Football, he argued persuasively in a smoky
jazz café, was the opium of the people. Where religion had
once held together socio-economic contradictions by telling
those who suffer under capitalism that their lot in life is
sanctioned by God and their reward would come in Heaven,
today football kept the masses happy. High unemployment
and a greater divide between the haves and have nots
ought to have resulted in an uprising, he said, but the
drug of football kept the brow-beaten content and, instead
of venting their anger in demonstrations and ultimately
revolution, these should-be malcontents were giving vent
to their emotions on the terraces. The obscenities shouted
at the officials ought to have been yelled at owners of the
means of production and the taunting of opposition players
was replacing a considered rejection of the bourgeois value

system. It was ridiculous, I know, but it seemed a more plausible theory back in Thatcher's Britain, and he was very good looking. So football went underground and for a time I felt guilty when I screamed in terror as Everton pressed for a late winner in the 90th minute. I was being manipulated, right? It is downright disgusting what an older man can do to a poor, impressionable girl.

I had no football pals but my girlfriends and family tolerated the obsession. Many a time my best friend would sit uncomplaining through a European match which for her must have embodied purgatory plus extra time. But now, as I stepped into adulthood, I was facing actual opposition, and I entered a desert where no one much liked football. This was a sad time, a time of going to the cinema, clubs and bars. Of tutorials on scientific theory, of finding notes in my cubby-hole which said 'You might also find an article by John Morrall in *Political Studies*, 1983 useful. It is partly a review of de Ste Croix.' Really. What about that goal at Stamford Bridge? What about that result at Old Trafford?

Needless to say a brief first post-university job in the fashion industry failed to offer fertile ground for a discussion on who was England's most skilful winger, but normal service was restored while in my next post. I worked for the *Pharmaceutical Journal* and met a girl who also liked football.

'Who do you support?'

'Liverpool.'

'Fantastic. Who's your favourite player?'

'I don't follow them as closely now. But my very favourites were Ray Clemence and Steve Heighway.'

'No kidding. Heighway is my all-time hero. I even wrote him letters.'

'So did I.'

'Yes, well, he wrote back to me.'

'Oh he wrote to me too.'

'Oh.'

At first I was jealous, of course. I had assumed Steve replied only to me, his most perceptive fan. But after glowering for a few days I saw Sue and I could be kindred spirits and swallowed my pride and went round for dinner.

Not long after one of the most significant events in my life occurred. I joined an insurance magazine. My first day was on a press day, which for a weekly magazine can be frantic, and there was no time for anything other than news writing. During the first quiet moment the following day when the phones had stopped ringing and everyone was sat at their desk, the news editor asked who I supported, in the sort of tone of voice normally reserved for 'Where were you on the night of the murder?'

'Liverpool.' There were a couple of sniggers from the back.

'Are you from Liverpool?'

'Yes.' No sniggers.

And slowly the sad, myopic, love of my life was laid bare. But there, in that office, it did not seem sad, it felt normal, requisite even. I pinned a photograph of the Liverpool team on the wall next to my desk. By the time I left that office, six years later, I had taken over an entire wall with my football memorabilia.

There was Sean, a West Bromwich Albion supporter, who was Irish and had seen Heighway play for the Republic. Sean let his observations on Heighway's 34 appearances for Ireland last over at least 34 separate trips to the pub.

Sean was not one to rush through his opinions and recollec-
tions but it was warming to hear tales of my hero I had not
heard before. There was Graham, a Sheffield Wednesday
fan and the most pleasant Tory you are ever likely to
encounter, who along with every other Wednesday fan I
have ever met, maintains a bleak pessimism as to his team's
fate before each season and each and every game. There
was Joe, a West Ham fan, who, the day after Liverpool
had been knocked out of the Coca-Cola Cup by his team,
hid under his desk and hummed *You'll Never Walk Alone* as
I walked dejectedly into the office. This was imaginative
but also highly determined as I was an hour and a half late
that morning. There was David, the boss, who supported
Tottenham but grindingly shifted his allegiance to Leyton
Orient and maintained a lofty demeanour when we told him
this was appalling behaviour.

And there was Bill who did not support anybody. Bill
found the football banter bemusing and boasted in his
desperately plummy voice that he had never seen a game
and was not ever likely to. 'Why don't you come to the
Giotto exhibition at the Tate instead, this soccer thing is
really rather ridiculous.'

We spent many hours compiling lists: footballers with reli-
gious surnames, a food and drink XI, players whose names
were also places, and during World Cups or European
Championships it was a wonder we produced a publication
at all. What with Joe sat fondling his dreadlocked wig in
honour of Holland and Ruud Gullit, and me trying to
memorise the names of the entire Russian squad as Sean
filled in our 'free with *Shoot*' wall-chart, a fly-on-the-wall
documentary would have been damning.

Then someone suggested we talked a good game but

how about playing it? There was much excitement. Where would we play, we were all unfit of course, would we find enough people for a game. And then Graham noticed I was bouncing up and down on my chair and with genuine concern said, 'You can't play.'

'Why not?'

'Well, I will feel uncomfortable if I tackle you, I might hurt you, you're a girl.'

'Well in that case you shouldn't play as you wear glasses and I shall feel uncomfortable when I dive in for a header and knock them to the floor and then accidentally trample on them – that is if they haven't smashed already and a sliver of glass has become lodged in your retina and we have to stop the match while we wait for an ambulance and then argue who is going to accompany you to Moorfields . . .'

'All right, all right, you can play.'

I would prefer to recall that conversation as one in which I did not squeal or stamp my foot and that my powers of reason swayed opinion but I have a horrible feeling I was allowed to join in because they all knew I would whinge and nag, and they would probably need me to make up the numbers anyway. Years later as we reminisced over the start of our big adventure Graham said a far better and more succinct retort to his opposition to my presence would have been 'Well then you can't play because you're shite.'

Between us we herded together 12 people prepared to trek over to Regent's Park after work. Someone from the advertising department brought a ball. I was not nervous, just excitable. I knew what I wanted to do, I wanted to run and dribble and cross. I had seen Steve Heighway do that enough times – latterly on videos of Liverpool's finest hours, a staple gift from Father Christmas – all I had to do was copy the technique. Unfortunately my lack of physical familiarity with a spherical leather-bound object took its toll and as the ball ricocheted off my knee-cap for the fifteenth time the dreamed of shouts of 'My God what a talent!' sounded suspiciously like 'My God what's that bloody woman doing here!'

It was a down-beat debut. It was quite possibly the worst debut Regent's Park had ever seen. The game lasted about an hour. In that hour I learned many things. I realised I could not play. I realised how badly I wanted to. I was astonished to learn that being sworn at for being 'crap' did not result in me storming off to the tube to get away from the scene of my humiliation as quickly as possible. Instead I racked my brains for a way to salvage something from the match and discovered that if I ran incessantly from defender to defender trying to force them into an error, my team-mates were, if not impressed, then at least grateful for the effort. All I managed to do in that first hour that was close to competent was sneak possession and lay the ball off to a colleague. And so, having achieved something, I was more keen than ever to keep on trying. If just one decent pass could make me feel fleetingly like I had just won the European Cup, then imagine how I would feel if I scored a goal or played a full match bereft of errors. Perhaps the one constant from that first real attempt is the optimism. I can fall into deep troughs of self-doubt but somehow, even when playing poorly and knowing it and hating the fact, I believe I can and will play better next time.

Perhaps everyone thought I would never show my face again, but I was hooked. So hooked that I surreptitiously started to check who would be turning up the following week. The ball had been close to flat, so I bought a pump.

Soon I was bringing the ball too. Soon I was doing all the boring stuff that, if it is not done, means a game is make-shift if it takes place at all. In return I snatched lessons before and after matches from the less chauvinistic participants. On that road to Damascus one particular blinded-by-the-light lesson involved being taught that a ball is moving as it travels towards you and so if you are to control it you have to be moving too. I mentioned this to a team-mate recently at which he looked astonished and insecure.

'Blimey, I didn't know that, no one ever told me that.'

But that was the point. If you have played football from a young age such matters are instinctive. And so for the next five years it was a conscious act on my part that when the ball thundered in my direction I would meet it with my leg pulling back so as to cushion the speed and take neater control.

There are some skills, though, that cannot be taught to anyone past 20. Sure, I could run with the ball if out wide, on my own, with no opponent near enough to tackle, but I could not and would not take a man on. This had a strange effect on my game. A deficiency was turned into an asset. So desperate was I to get rid of the ball as soon as I received it that I became truly masterful at one-touch distribution. A typical move would find me, unmarked – at that time no bloke had the guts to be seen marking a woman – in the inside-left or right channel. I would be passed to and either instantly lay the ball off into the path of the chap who had passed initially and had kept on running, or I would spot someone else in space and slide it to them. It was, for a long time, the only positive thing I could do but allied to my effort and enthusiasm was just enough to ensure my presence was tolerable. Occasionally one of the guys who had been most cruel in the early weeks would mutter a word of praise or encouragement. By the end of that first summer when two 'captains' would pick a side, taking turns to pluck from the huddle of assembled talent, I was not always the last to be chosen.

There was absolutely no sense in which I was striking a blow for feminism. I felt honoured to be involved and took on all the donkey work uncomplainingly. At times I believed I was the only one who realised quite how wonderful it all was. Regent's Park was, and is, lovely. To emerge from the squalor of the Underground, where commuters' sweat mingles as their arm-pits stretch to find something to hold onto and the air grows thin as trains become stranded for minutes that feel like months in between stations, and find the peace of the park was in itself a joy. For, without football, none of us would have travelled to the park for the sake of it. You either go home or go home after a visit to the pub next to the office, and home is rarely as idyllic as Regent's Park late on a sultry afternoon.

Then came the routine pitch-grabbing. The sunnier the day, the less room there was. Whoever arrived first had to try to set up two goals with their one bag and make it look as if a game would start at any moment. Participants arrived in little gangs. If we were not in our usual spot, it was not unheard of for colleagues to become disorientated and wander off in the wrong direction having mistaken a distant silhouette for someone they knew. At such times my presence was invaluable. I had worn for my first game a dull, lost-its-colour-in-the-wash T-shirt but within months of realising that this park life was the highlight of my week, I had taken to investing in replica club and country kits. All a lost player had to do was skirt the horizon for my wild mop of hair and garish shirt. It became customary for those travelling separately to phone to find out which shirt I would be wearing. Complete strangers would shout my name. They were friends of friends who had been told to look for the girl in the Barcelona/Liverpool/Norway shirt.

I suppose I was exceptionally lucky at the level of tolerance. I had a quite appalling tendency to regard the whole weekly escapade as mine. I turned up every week. I never said 'I don't feel like it' because I had a cold, or a date, or work to finish off. I phoned around to ensure enough people would turn up and issued stern rebukes if anyone broke his word. I glared at anyone who left early or turned up late. I obsessively measured the distance between the bags or umbrellas that counted as goalposts and cajoled those who wanted to keep their jumper on to take it off if it meant we had the right number of white shirts to play against red and blue ones.

If someone sounded hesitant about turning up I gave them the Ally Lecture:

'When else are you going to be able to play with people who play because they love football and don't hack into you? It is a privilege to be asked. You are privileged to be able-bodied. It is a chance to get fit, to relive the days when you dreamed of playing for United. It is a chance to play a team sport without giving up your entire Sunday just to sit on the bench with a group of blokes you don't know and don't like and who think the offside trap is the whole bloody point.'

I have never asked why they all put up with me. Maybe they thought it was hilarious and I missed the joke. I brought the pump and the adapter but would casually throw them over to whoever mentioned they had noticed the ball needed air. One day I was the one who noticed. I fiddled and meddled and generally struggled to work the pump. I became aware of a wide-eyed audience.

'What are you trying to do? Haven't you ever pumped up a ball before?'

'Er, no.'

'What about your bike, when you had a flat tyre as a kid you must have pumped that up.'

'Er, no. I always got my dad to do it.'

For some reason my lack of experience with a pump and the subsequent lesson were regarded with awe-struck incredulity and a wedge of crude humour. Many of the guys acted as if it were this incident and this alone which alerted them to the fact I was female. But once I had learned how there was no stopping me. Curiously it was not something the lads ever felt able to let go of and even though I had pumped the ball, one of them had to test it and add just a couple more spurts for good measure, give the ball a final squeeze and sigh knowingly before whacking it into the middle distance. That was another male/female thing. I have never had the urge to kick the ball towards nothing in particular. It is rather like a dog lifting its leg when it has run out of piss. It makes a statement but it is a pretty fruitless one.

That first summer in the park represented to me what back-packing around the world means to some others. It was what I had always wanted to do but had never had the chance to. I was so enveloped by the desire to join in that I did not worry about those lads who never passed the ball to me. Indeed, I was extremely grateful to be passed to more than twice per match. For the rest of the time I harried and relied on interceptions. A rebound near the goal allowed me a shot or two. Afterwards I would pester my work colleagues about my technique and ask for another quick lesson or a nugget of advice.

That first summer I never once called for a pass, never took a set-piece and never dribbled past anyone. I did win the odd tackle and score from the penalty spot, however, and that gave me something to dwell on and gloat over as I soaked in the bath later in the evening. Bruises appeared, beautiful, oval, green and black signs of proof of commitment. 'Look,' I would command, as I rolled up my trousers or peeled back my skirt knowing full well but ignoring the fact that this was how five-year-olds treat cuts and bruises.

When it was cold, fewer people turned up for our game and for the other matches in the park. When it poured with rain only our team turned up. The park was transformed from a regal thoroughfare of delight for tourists and dog owners and families into a desolate, empty swamp. It was impossible to play properly as no one could stay on their feet longer than three seconds. They could have if they had wanted to, but this was a chance to splash, skid and wallow in mud that many among us thought had gone once adulthood arrived. Those first forays to the park were made in the main by men who had not played football since college or school. We all tried diving headers and bicycle kicks when it rained because the ground was softer than our beds and because in those conditions no errors were ridiculed. We just laughed and sploshed and splashed and grinned knowingly at each other when our fair-weather friends turned up a sunny fortnight later.

Sometimes there would be only six or seven of us standing forlornly next to the children's playground.

'Who else is coming Ally?'

But no one else came. I would seethe, making a mental note to castigate the culprits who would later come up with too much work, forgetting their shorts, a stag party or girlfriend problems in mitigation, but never 'Mind your own bloody business, I'll play when I can'. And that could only mean that deep down everyone knows the importance of football.

When we were low on bodies one solution was to accept a couple of park stragglers who had asked to join in. Park stragglers are remarkable. Some have been turning up for the full ten years I have and still they cannot find a team willing automatically to include them, to adopt them as part of their group. This is partly because they are odd characters with no humour and an inflated sense of what they can bring to a game, and partly because they want to stay on the outside. They are football mercenaries. They would rather football was an individual sport, but as it is a team game the best they can hope for is to maintain an aloofness and a belief that they are needed. Without them the game would crumble, they think.

The most famous Regent's Park Straggler is Tony. Tony always, always, wears a Napoli shirt. He is Italian, short, slightly bow-legged and is greying. He has a thick accent and tends to avoid eye contact. The first time we came across him we were pleased to do so for we badly needed an extra player. But that is the worst occasion on which to meet Tony. He ranted, he swore. He took all the corners and stood in sarcastic astonishment, arms outstretched when no one scored from them. He would hold on to the ball for far too long, then perform his little tricks on the wing and then berate us for not making the runs he wanted us to.

Tony never asks for a game. He uses a sort of soccer osmosis which involves finding him slap, bang in the middle of the space you are about to use for a match. For a while, even when we had plenty of players, we would let Tony join us. After all the spirit of park football is to embrace anyone desperate for a game. But gradually we feared catching sight of the blue shirt for we knew there would be periods in the match when we might as well sit on the ground, pull open a can and fill out a pools coupon for all the actual football Tony was going to allow us to play.

In the end we took to telling him we had enough people. It did not seem to bother him, no doubt he thinks it is our loss, and we have become the very last group he will attempt to grace with his skills. The fear lives on though, and now and again one of us spots a Napoli-clad figure in the middle distance and should it hover near new-found friends who do not know the full Tony trauma we have to race over to them, whereupon they are bemused by our paranoia and lack of generosity.

There are jollier types of perennial straggler. There is Steve, a giant of a man, whom I had coincidentally met at LSE. He laughed his huge Frank Bruno-style belly laugh when he first saw me in the park and has done so more or less ever since. When we first knew each other Steve ran a college radio station and I had been involved in a spoof interview as a wind-up at the expense of one unsuspecting, poor mature student. It involved some pretty ghastly undergraduate humour, and, unfortunately, Steve remembered it all. For that reason I have never told Steve we do not need his services, although he does suffer from the stragglers' disease of hogging the ball. Steve will play with one group until they quit and then move on to another, impervious to the fact they may be nearing the end of a finely balanced match and definitely do not need, or want, a sudden extra player. By that stage Steve is usually sweating profusely and complaining that he cannot run far. It is like turning up late for a dinner party you were not properly invited to and complaining that you have already eaten too much elsewhere but you will force yourself to scoff the chocolate meringue.

And there are the sad stragglers. Without bravado it can be difficult to find a game and so some guys never do. Once we were up and running with about seven-a-side when a man in a business suit, spruce white shirt and paisley tie came and stood two or three feet from our goal. He was carrying a sports bag, but I did not recognise him and over the next ten minutes or so I tried to ask as many of our team as possible if he was a friend of theirs. No one seemed to know who he was. If we had been short of a player I would have asked him if he wanted a game but the match was just about perfect and there was no call to unbalance it. This man bided his time and then methodically undressed, put on his football boots, his shorts and T-shirt and folded up his suit. And then, five minutes or so later, without moving nearer or farther or talking to anyone, he took off all his kit, put his suit back on and slowly walked away. I could not quite believe he had wanted to be asked to play and had not the guts to ask for himself, but there seemed no other plausible explanation. It is a cruel life, this park life.

CHAPTER FOUR

my blokes and other babes

It is rather poetic and so unlikely for strangers to mingle and learn to smile together in the cold, unfeeling metropolis but in football it happens: some stragglers evolve into regulars. We have picked up players who knew none of us to begin with but who, by turning up hopeful of a match at the same place and at the same time as we do, have been assimilated. It is taking it too far, however, when the stranger starts to bring his mates along as well. We need to feel there is a kernel of family, of founder members and their friends. We do not want to lose our identity, our vague but keenly clung-to philosophy that we play the beautiful, passing game where it is as joyous to have been part of a move that led to a goal as it is to score one.

The stragglers' reaction to there being a woman involved varies. Initially the reaction is similar; if they let a woman play, they can hardly object to a straggler asking for a game, and quite probably we are pestered more than most as a consequence. And they are all fairly bemused that I have a say in whether they should join in or not.

'What do you think Ally? Are we expecting anyone else? What should we do?'

This is the reaction more because it allows my team-mates

to deflect any possible confrontation and it saves them calculating how uneven the sides are, than a reflection on my power and status. But new players do not know this and never, ever, say anything sexist. The desire to play football represents a far stronger urge than the suspicion of women and to my knowledge no man has ever turned on his heels because I am there.

I suspect stragglers or newcomers wonder if they are about to witness some female reincarnation of Pelé, a woman who has played in Italy, perhaps in a professional league, a woman who outpaces everyone on the park and attracts camera crews and photo-journalists with her scissors-kick routine and somersault celebrations. It saddens me that I have to let them down.

So, politely, the strangers join in. And they politely never pass to me once. Or they go slightly overboard and deliver far more excellent balls to my feet or head than I actually deserve. One recent summer found me suffering a dip in form that left my oldest and dearest footie pals neglecting to pass to me. And then along came Mike, a straggler, and a very good player, who would pass to me whenever he possibly could. So, even when we have too many participants, I maintain he has a right to play with us. Not quite a cash-for-questions type of corruption, but sad, self-interested behaviour all the same.

There has been a slight but perceptible change in the attitudes of strangers to my presence over the past ten years. In the beginning men were either suspicious or terribly accommodating in a patronising sort of way. There were, and still are, and always will be, men who cannot bring themselves to pass a ball to a woman, but overall there is an acceptance that I have a right to be part of the game, or at the least that they have no right to bar me. The silly comments have practically dried up. There was a time when on top of my lack of natural ability I had to suffer 'Oi darlin' watch how you chest that ball down.' It is more likely now that, if a bloke thinks that, he will also think better of saying it.

Perhaps this shift away from sexism has something to do with me. I am more relaxed about my football. I am less excitable, bossy and over-keen and instead more confident, laid back and fatalistic. I am therefore less obvious. I am less pretty, too, and I am sure that is more acceptable. Deep down men prefer not to play with women who are too obviously attractive and not too masculine either.

For myself, if I am engaged in a game of football in the park with men, I prefer it to stay that way. If another woman joins then she has to be a certain sort. For a while this was a gut instinct and I did not dwell on it because I assumed I was being possessive and I did not care to have that verified. But I have played alongside varying types of women in mainly male games and I have discovered that there is a strange logic to my attitude. The basic tenet is that I feel honoured, privileged, or certainly fortunate to be part of this male domain and I am worried that if the female angle is pushed too far I will be rejected; a case of throwing the baby out with the bath water, throwing the blonde out with the irritating babes.

In the early days a girl from work or a girlfriend of one of our gang would, albeit rarely, ask to join in. There seemed no basis on which to deny this request. After all, I played, and none too well at that. But it was wrong. It was so horribly wrong. They would squeal. They would run with their arms outstretched as if holding a skipping rope. They did not work hard. If they were at fault for a goal they chuckled. Above all else my problem with this was that my individuality would suffer and the guys would stop seeing me as Ally and start seeing me as The Other Sex, as just another damned woman. I did not want to risk alienating my team. They had enough to put up with seeing me veering towards them every week, extra squeaking femininity might strain their tolerance.

I will not deny I was afraid that one of these women would exhibit, despite being a football virgin, the poise and skill I lacked and thus push me further down the pecking order of soccer low-life. But the main fear was being outed.

'Look we're sorry, *Alyson*, but this is a bloke thing, we don't go around forcing our way onto netball courts. You'll have to stop pestering us.'

I dreaded those words but I never heard them, not within earshot at least.

If a woman is a very good, experienced player and takes the game seriously, then I can cope, but even then I would not and do not think it would be fair for there to be too many women at any one time playing in a match that had begun as a men's affair. I am too afraid of the repercussions.

One other girl has become a Regent's Park part-timer and she poses no threat to the status quo. She is the sister of one of the more gifted and likeable blokes and she plays at a high women's league level. Samantha is faster, younger and fitter than I, and has benefited from learning the game at a younger age with encouragement from a sibling. She is quiet and shy off the field but vociferous on it. The lads praise any impressive cross or tackle she makes in much the same way as they encourage me, but what many of them find difficult is her recent tendency to become so involved that she cajoles them. She directs who the sweeper should pass to and gently admonishes if her advice is not heeded. She will say 'good effort' if a player slices a shot and then say 'well played' if they get the next shot on target.

I have seen Tom, our fifty-something libero, glower and seethe when he has been the butt of her good nature. Not many of the guys have the nerve to offer advice to Tom. He is terribly important, I am led to believe, in the world of academia and law, and an astounding talent on the pitch. He is therefore, and quite understandably, our maestro, our admiral. He calls everyone 'darling' and gets away with it. Some of the team are also academic lawyers and naturally bow to his superiority, some have nothing whatsoever to do with him outside of football and occasionally find him pompous but all the same take the advice he gives because he is usually right.

Samantha does not know us socially, however, and has little knowledge or regard for this complex power structure. It is her temerity rather than her femininity that annoys Tom and for that reason I find it funny and not a worrying trend that is liable to throw my own acceptance into jeopardy.

I have played in games with equal numbers of men and women. These were not organised by me and I did not know any of the men very well. I was an outsider and not at all bothered how the men felt about playing alongside women. In any case it was safe to assume they were in favour because they had been invited by their sister or a female friend or their partner, and the basis for each of these games was to give us particularly keen girls, all already in a women's team, some additional practice when a women's league game had been cancelled or the season was at an end.

My approach to these games was unusual. Because the bulk of my football experiences had been alongside men, I was highly relaxed where some of the women were slightly nervous. I had a sense of superiority, that this was old hat for me and would be easier because men, and I, know more about the game. This was disgusting but I could not help it. I was being sexist. I knew how men played, I knew how women played and when the women are not of a terribly high standard their footballing instincts are undeveloped when compared to men, no matter what level the men play at. Unfortunately, I play to the best of my ability when I feel arrogant. And so I scored with dipping 30-yard shots, played nifty one-twos, dribbled around three at a time and was generally a little show-off. Although in mitigation I would add that, when I show off, it is still a meek display by the standards of most consistent and practised show-offs.

And because these were other women's men, my popularity among those women nose-dived. I could see annoyance, jealousy and distaste in their eyes as their men-folk praised my efforts. Perhaps odder still, I did not really like these games. They were not serious enough. All-women league games are serious and so are the all-men games that I infiltrate. This was too knock-about for me which, of course, must only have served to increase my apparent arrogance and the contempt in which I was held. I dare say some of the women thought I was flirting or there was some kind of courtship at the heart of this behaviour but there was none. Indeed, I would normally have been far more interested in gaining the friendship of the girls and avoiding conflict with them, but on these occasions some other instinct, not mating, took over. It was a football heritage. I shared more values and experiences with the men than with the women and if they wanted mixed football they could have it, but they had better not think all women are the same.

I have never noticed any sexual chemistry during a match between players. There is instead the chemistry of intuition which can be struck with the most unlikely of characters and there is favouritism. Favouritism has more to do with longevity of friendship, or of being related, than fancying a player. Sean invited his old buddy from schooldays along to the second ever match we played in Regent's Park and ever since Sean has been more likely to pass to Conor and Conor more likely to pass to Sean should there be two or three alternatives open to them. This I am sure is because they are temporarily transported back to their youth and it is an instinctive act of loyalty. All the same we try to split them up if we can.

The bath water theorem was settled for me when Samantha brought along Kerry, a team-mate from her ladies side and a woman I had interviewed for *The Times* a few years earlier because she had been capped many times for England. I was not threatened by Kerry's presence, I was thrilled. She probably could have done without me whispering to everyone, 'She's an England international you know,' but no one was at all impressed.

'Yes?'

'Is she?'

'How good is she?'

'Oh, I didn't notice she was a woman.'

That was the sum total of the chaps' response. But for me it was an honour. I had watched quite a few England games and been impressed by the girls' commitment – they have to plead for time off work to represent their country.

Although their performances were far from polished, there were gifted and strong players to admire. I was pleased that we ended up, all three girls, on the same side. Usually Sam and I are on opposite sides as though it is necessary, subliminally, to even out the hormone levels of the teams. But here was I passing and being passed to by one of the best woman players in the country. Maybe she was having an off day, but the gulf was not so great. She had a wicked, powerful shot and confidence of manner when in control of the ball that gave away her background, but beyond that there was not much to separate us. More to the point she played the game without any hint of superiority or overt femininity. She was a player who did not let women, and, subsequently, me down.

Men have.

I became friends with Gareth at LSE. He was spotty, wore unflattering spectacles and had greasy, limp hair. He had a crush on a student and asked me, out of the blue in the middle of the street, what he should do about it and himself. I was honest. I told him to wear contacts, wash his face, get his hair cut at a trendy salon and buy his clothes in Covent Garden. I never expected to talk to him again. But a week later he tapped me on the shoulder and smirked. He was transformed. Gareth had, in the space of six days, become a cocky, style conscious, good-looking babe magnet. To me he was still Gareth and we still went to the bridge club together, but he got his girl and was never insecure again.

In fact I had unwittingly created a monster. At first I admired the fact he still wanted to hang out with the girl who knew his secret and I forgave his displays of arrogance as a blip on his path of self-discovery but gradually I realised that there was no stopping him, his confidence was growing exponentially. After graduating he joined a firm that had buildings opposite my office and so it was inevitable that he would tag along one day with me to Regent's Park. Inevitable that he would tell me he was a fantastic player, inevitable that he would be talented. But what was worse and not so predictable, although nonetheless not too surprising, was that he would analyse, unasked, my team-mates' strengths and weaknesses.

'I'd say, you are basically a good player, Sean, but you need to . . .' I went deaf from dumbfoundness. I watched Sean's face as he struggled to avoid apoplexy.

'Well, we all have areas where we can improve our game,' Sean said and moved to the other side of the pub. I had known Sean for four years by then and had not once dared even to consider offering a critique of any aspect of his life. Sean has a very gentle authority, particularly when dealing with anyone younger than himself. Without saying a word he conveys the impression to me that he knows his and your foibles but would rather not know your opinion about either.

I was grateful Sean avoided some scathing put-down and it would have had to have been vitriolic to have got under Gareth's skin. Gareth turned to me after Sean had moved away and said he was glad Sean had accepted and understood the advice. Later Sean said he was lenient because he was not sure how good a friend of mine Gareth was. At around this point Gareth ceased to be Gareth and became known as Aston Villa.

Usually it is a loveable trait to be a devout fan of a club. There are many of us park footballers who wear replica kit and know all there is to know about Birmingham City, Chelsea or Newcastle United. But Aston Villa knew Aston

Villa were superior. He could not accept his view might be tainted by his fondness for them. Real fans see their team's vulnerability and are if anything over-critical because they are so desperate for success and a style to be proud of. Real fans are allowed to detest rival clubs but they must guard themselves against disappointment by considering actual or potential failings within their team. No one took to Aston Villa's kind of support and, fortunately, he became so important in his new job that he could not play football with us any more. It took me several weeks to recover from the appraisal he made of my own soccer skills.

There are many permutations of park football. Sometimes there are no stragglers to make up the numbers and we have to join forces with an entire team. The level of negotiation this involves is extraordinary. For a start there is a general unwillingness to ask at all but, since I am the most keen to ensure our trip to the park is as fruitful as possible, I end up making the initial tentative enquiries as to whether the other team wants to expand. It has been so desperate that I have sprinted circuitous miles in search of a group prepared to share their patch of turf.

'How many of you are there?' they might say.

'Seven,' I might say.

'Well, we can take three of you, no more.'

Of course this is unacceptable. All for one, and one for all, and all that. Occasionally the effort of asking around yields the near perfect solution of finding another group of seven and we contest an evenly fought game. One such find came in Year Three. I found a group of graphic designers for us to play with and it resulted in an understanding that we would always play against each other when possible. Eventually both our groups shrank and combined to be a single entity. About once a year we reminisce about this marriage. I remind everyone that it was me, Ally, who first asked the designers' leader, Nick, if we could play with them and every year the guys say 'Really?' and they genuinely have forgotten that we were two groups of strangers who met on the grass one evening.

It is sometimes the case that we have to join another group because of lack of park space. We have suffered some ridiculous 15-a-side games, that while better than nothing, are about as far removed from the beautiful game as you can get while there is still a football involved. But it is during these contests that male opponents mind most if I get the better of them. For them, the more participants the grander the stage, and I have seen men's faces collapse in anger and humiliation as I dispossess them and if that tiny, rare piece of Ally magic should result in a goal, they curse and snarl and then do one of two things. They either make sure that the next time I try to tackle them, they attempt a drag-back and a sudden surge of pace, just to put me in my place and let everyone know the previous incident was a fluke, or they avoid me altogether, scared of what to be seen publicly outwitted by a woman will do to their credibility.

Football used to be so much a man's world. I even have sympathy with men who liked the fact that going to a match or playing in one was something they could do without women with them or near them. I have been on girls' nights out and can understand how the presence of a member of the opposite sex can alter the tone. The whole notion that football wants families and women must irk many blokes and make them feel hunted on what used to be well protected territory. So, I am always genuinely touched when a man says 'Well played', or admits he came off second best. Most of those guys I have been playing against for many years do not consciously think about the fact they are about to tackle a girl. Instead I think they have absorbed my strengths and weaknesses in the same way as they have with the other, male, players, and if some of those weaknesses are as a consequence of my sex then they are not being sexist any more than they are being heightist or fattist when assessing other team-mates.

At our Christmas party Lionel was describing a recent five-a-side game and said, 'You know how it is, when you're about to tackle Ally you expect whoever it is to come out of the tackle with the ball, but in that game no one did, I remember I didn't.' It was decent of him to acknowledge I had been impressive but what struck me more was the notion that he and the team had an image of how I play. I did not realise that the fact that it is usually easy to take the ball off me was known. I sort of assumed that when I made up for it by tackling back or winning the ball off someone else a few minutes later, I had redressed the balance. I naïvely took every game in isolation and because my performances are so variable I assumed that until the next match, I was regarded as good, bad or indifferent.

Compliments and encouragement after a game are a bonus, during a match they are my lifeblood. That I receive more than most is not patronising. Ridiculous though it may seem, I am quite rightly regarded as a player who is still learning, still hoping to improve. I have noticed how I receive more praise in the immediate aftermath of a particularly embarrassing gaffe than after I have scored with a stunning volley. This applies to all the players but is exaggerated for me, the wannabe.

I have sometimes performed so badly that there is nothing

anyone can say, but usually a team-mate finds something positive to talk about. Because I am so desperate to take something positive from a match I had been looking forward to all day I can by-pass the rules that would apply in other realms of life, such as feeling insulted if complimented on the shape of my toenail when I am wearing a new and expensive dress or if praised for the length of an article when I had hoped it was well-written.

What sums up the relationship between my team and me is the card they sent after I broke my foot. No one else sent a card, no girlfriends, or office pals. But my team signed an A to Z of Football card. Someone asterisked that A was also for Ally and the comments were of the 'come back we can't organise the games without you' variety, but Russell wrote that they were missing my silky skills. And the phrase silky skills was in inverted commas.

For all my tiny triumphs, occasionally lovely goals and scything passes, I am still the one who has yet to attain the status of a real footballer. I will get there though.

CHAPTER FIVE

Italia 90 and the prize

Year Two of park football coincided with the 1990 World Cup finals. This was so exciting that the whole personality of Regent's Park was changed, irrevocably so. Hazy memories of World Cups of our youth were redundant. The fever of Italia 90 rekindled a passion for football that many men assumed they had lost forever. It also stirred the souls of many of those, mainly women, who had hitherto been immune to soccer.

I acknowledged the changes as they were happening. With a zeal more intense than that of any born-again preacher I exploited Italia 90. I sucked it dry. The bottom line was that I would make my home a party zone, more fun to be at than Italy itself, but the catch was you could not join in unless you opened your heart to football. 'Football is knocking at the door of your soul, let it in.'

I was in my element. I had just entered the peak phase of buying football boot after football boot and football shirt after football shirt and now I could let rip. I found two immense, giant tablecloth-sized Italian flags and I hung them from the first floor windows of my tiny terraced house. The downstairs windows I plastered full with cut-outs of favourite players, ensuring a lively mix of nationalities were represented. It meant no daylight entered the house but it did not seem to matter. You cannot watch football on TV with sunlight invading the room anyway. It crossed my mind that my neighbours might complain. They had already expressed disgust that my front garden was overgrown, one neighbour even inventing a story about a giant rat that had jumped out of my garden and attacked her throat in order to prompt me into action. And they were elderly. Many had lived in the same east London street all their lives, still had a parlour and brown nicotine-stained ceilings. They would not take kindly to one of the houses being turned into a theme park. I would stand at the end of the street on leaving it and on re-entering it and just gaze in wonder and joy at my Little Italy, its billowing flags and the red, green and white bunting I had stretched from the front door to the garden wall. But I hurried once I neared my home, fearing a lengthy confrontation with an indignant neighbour. I need not have worried. There were no complaints and, touchingly, when a flag became dislodged, which they did frequently, a neighbour would fold it up and post it back through my door. They probably thought I was of Italian descent and pitied me so far from home.

Inside the house was more glorious still. Every team in the World Cup was represented by a huge rosette and each nation's fortunes were represented by how far up my wall they were positioned. I had hated the textured wallpaper that covered the house, that I could not afford nor be bothered to replace, but now it came into its own as I could pin the rosettes straight on to it. There were charts galore, stickers, posters, scarves and more flags. And there were menus. I issued invitations to watch specific matches and listed on the invitation what I would be cooking. The meals related to the team I wanted to win. So there was beef stroganoff followed by vodka and lemon mousse for Russia v Argentina, Spanish omelettes for Spain v Belgium, Spaghetti carbonara and supermarket tiramisu for Italy v Austria and cannabis cake for Holland v Egypt. The cake was brought by a friend. For the famous England v Germany semi-final I laid out a fine English spread and included cucumber sandwiches and good old English trifle but it did not influence the outcome, and so for the final I was forced into supporting Germany on the basis that Argentina had been so sullen and unsporting. The food was brought in by a gang of Germans my sister knew and they spent hours over my little gas stove only to produce, ten minutes into the game, some nasty frankfurters and sauerkraut. Less appetising still was their muted patriotism. 'We know we will win, we do not need to shout about it,' was their explanation.

My enthusiasm for this World Cup was contagious. There may have been friends and colleagues who thought I was unbearable but I did not notice them. Rather, I noted how my invitations, complete with menu, details of the match and eating times as well as kick-off times, were coveted by those who were not offered one. One girl made little chirruping noises: 'Can't I come along to one of these parties?' I sighed. I told her there were not *parties*, they were only for people who loved football and I had assumed, as she did not know the difference between Preston North End and the Leeds–Liverpool Canal, that she would not enjoy herself. 'Oh but I will, I like big tournaments.' So she received her invite. But it was as I had feared and 20 minutes into the match she started to swing her legs as she sat on an uncomfortable high backed chair and clicked her tongue against the roof of her mouth, 'Is this all we are going to do, watch football?'

Once the World Cup was over Regent's Park became quieter, but even on damp days it was more full with amateur footballers than it would have been previously. My team swelled and consolidated. My presence became less harrowing and I was on my way to becoming a fixture, something the boys could take for granted, like the occasional dog turd on the grass or perhaps a dandelion.

At length I found myself balking at interviewing yet another insurance broker for my magazine. I was competent at my job and even began to be generously remunerated for it, but slowly, ever so gradually, an idea was forming. It was a calling, or at least you could name it that if I had been drawn to nursing or to the sea. Whatever it was, it was strong. I did not care how unlikely it sounded, I had to make football my job. Occasionally I would tell someone what I had decided and then add that my one reservation was that if football was how I earned my money I might not love it so much. I do not know why I said this. I also frequently say that winning lots of money ruins your life and I believe this to be true so I do not ever enter the National Lottery. But for me football is the equivalent of the Lottery in other people's lives and I refuse to accept you can have too much of it.

I was not blinded with optimism, I knew it would be very difficult. I had worked briefly with a woman who became a high-profile financial journalist on a national daily. She told me she wanted to switch to the sports desk but they would not let her. She had then fixed me with her stare and said, ever so sombrely with the air of a woman who knows for certain we are being taken over by alien life forms: 'You can never change disciplines, they won't let you.' Her words deterred me for an afternoon. She may not have tried hard enough, I thought.

I figured there were two ways in. You know someone or you get lucky. I did not know anyone and luck? You make your own luck. And then someone, I cannot remember who, because the second they told me I knew this was the way and I had become very excited, told me the *Observer* was running a charity auction. Various items had been put up for this auction, tea with Robin Cook was one of them, and readers sent in bids, not knowing how high or low they would prove to be, but it was not supposed to matter because all of it went to charity. It did not matter to me because the prize I was bidding for was about to create a footballing miracle. The prize was a trip to Anfield to meet the players in the players' lounge. I could meet my heroes and then write about the experience. Once my piece was published I could send it to all the sports editors in the land and then be offered a job. Simple. I cackled myself to sleep.

The prize was for two. I immediately thought of Sue, the girl who had also written to Steve Heighway. I thought of her because she shared my intoxication for the Pool and because she was a best mate, but also I think I thought of her because I knew she could afford to bump up the amount we needed to bid in order to win the jackpot. We engaged in a breathless, hurried conversation over the phone.

'Sue, do you want to meet the players, in the players' lounge?'

'Ooh, yes.'

'How much would you pay for that?'

We briskly assessed, after I had explained the rules, how much we should offer. We did not stop to wonder if we could afford it, we wondered only who we might be up against. We decided that the chances that someone who was very wealthy who also read the *Observer* who was also an avid Liverpool fan who would have seen the offer were slim. But, by the same token we did not want to run the risk of losing out. So we bid £400.

The *Observer* phoned me at work to tell me I had won the trip to Anfield. 'In fact,' said the caller, 'you bid quite a lot more than anyone else.'

'Well, it's for charity isn't it?' I retorted, sounding far more cheesed off than I intended. Our prize was organised by one of the big sports manufacturers. I shall call them Addibok, and all our planning had to go through them. Once a date was set, I telephoned the *Observer* sports department whereupon a highly protective but not unpleasant secretary said the top writers in her office would 'go mad' if I was allowed to write a piece and she gave me the name of a features editor. Undeterred I ploughed on. After I explained my proposed article to the woman in charge of features, there was a pause. 'Tell me again, why this has something to do with the *Observer*,' she said. I said it was their charity auction and of course my piece would underline what a fantastic idea the auction was in the first place. That seemed to clinch it. In a dismissive voice, the features editor said she would send a photographer with us to Anfield and pay me £300. Three hundred? I would get my initial outlay back and end up in profit. Better not tell Sue.

The big day arrived. Sue and I had been holed up with my parents. We were so nervous we tagged along to a Women's Institute open day and bought some jam and Sue bought my mum some flowers. 'That Sue, she's lovely isn't she?'

my mother still says. Before we set off we had lunch in a pub but could not eat anything. As mum and dad waved us goodbye it was as if we were off to our first day at school. We were both trembling and relieved we had each other. The whole escapade had gone to my head. Never before had a photographer been dispatched just for me, and so I cast aside my replica shirt and jeans and put on a suit, with a short skirt, and my fake fur coat. I argued that you had to look smart to get in the players' lounge but really I was being vain.

Naturally the photographer had no trouble picking us out from the horde milling around the Shankly Gates. He wanted to take a picture of me stood on the pitch and I agreed wholeheartedly, perhaps even desperately, that this was an inspired idea. But the club refused permission. Clubs are very sniffy about who can stand on their pitch and yet think nothing of sharing it with a whole destructive rugby team week in week out. He took my picture outside the Gates instead. I felt partly ludicrous and horribly separate from the normal footballing experience and partly terribly important.

We sat in the main stand with a representative of Addibok. He was very pleasant and slightly nervous. We were watching Liverpool v Chelsea. Chelsea had not won at Anfield for some 600 years so we sat back relaxed in the knowledge we would see our team thump the Londoners. Liverpool lost. Sue, who has gentle blonde curls, rosy cheeks and round blue eyes, made Mr Addibok squirm in surprise at her side as a stream of expletives issued from her lips.

'They're not going to want to meet us now are they?' she asked me.

We hung around in the main foyer after the match. The

girl guarding the entrance to the players' section had not heard about two women with a date with the team and told us to go away. Mr Addibok wanted to know if we would accept free merchandise instead of meeting the players. My whole future flashed before my eyes. 'No,' I said, 'you get us in there. Look, ask Bruce Grobbelaar, he'll be in a good mood.' Bruce had saved a penalty and was one of the few Pool players to have emerged with any credit that afternoon. Sure enough he waved us through and we entered a corridor. As we did so a door slammed shut with real venom. I could almost smell that the manager Graeme Souness was behind that door and had bawled at some chosen players for their appalling efforts. And then the door to the players' lounge itself was opened. I had dwelt upon this moment for some time. The image that repeatedly presented itself was of a luxurious and spacious room with a sunken floor area. The wood panelling would be white, the carpets, a pinkish red. The effect was that of a James Bond film set, all slightly dated, slightly tasteless, but opulent.

The reality was somewhat different. I had taken the phrase 'players' lounge' far too literally and had been expecting soft sofas, deep pile carpets and cocktail shakers. Instead Sue and I trooped into a cramped and dingy and airless room. The chairs were plastic or schooldays wood, the tables cast-offs from an old people's home. There were even chairs placed along the wall in the best doctor's waiting room style. The bar itself was untidy and limited. Mr Addibok brought Sue and I some orange juice. He knew some of the players, but not all, and searched for someone he knew well enough to allow an introduction. He spotted Mark Wright. 'Ah, Mark, these two young ladies won a competition to meet all the players.' But Mark Wright stared past us into the middle distance, his cheeks flushed and his eyes moist, still, I assumed, dwelling on the dressing down he must have received from his boss, and muttered 'That's nice' just that bit too sarcastically to merit attempting further conversation. Mr Addibok squirmed once more and melted into the little room's bustle.

There was nothing for it but to be brave. I interrupted conversations, made interesting and pertinent comments that probably sounded like tiresome small talk. I overdid it. 'Are you a journalist?' asked Paul Elliott, with the Chelsea contingent. 'Er, yes, how did you guess that?' 'It's the way you talk, keep on asking questions, you're very direct.' But it worked. I met practically everyone. Dennis Wise had won the man of the match award and was clutching it as a child does a new doll. John Barnes was modest and pleasant, Jan Molby shy but nice, Michael Thomas' wife/girlfriend did not appreciate it when in answer to my question 'Where exactly is the hamstring?' he ran his finger down my thigh. Sue and I have recalled that moment approximately 257 times since.

Then the photographer burst in on the room. He had spent 40 minutes trying to convince security he was involved in a charity promotion event and was looking harassed. He wanted to take a photograph of me standing underneath the famous 'This is Anfield' sign above the tunnel. He wanted two players to stand there with me. Ronnie Rosenthal laughed and said he did not mind but that his English was poor. Dean Saunders was more reluctant but sheepishly agreed. I peeked into the changing room on the way. There was a platter of untouched sandwiches and still the reek of professional sweat. I made a mental note that teams probably do not feel like eating when they have just lost.

Then it was over. We waved goodbye to Mr Addibok, ate in Liverpool's China Town and nodded hello to some of the players again in the nightclubs. Back home I wrote my career-shattering piece, sent it to the commissioning editor and then phoned to find out what she thought. 'Yes, I've read it.' She paused. 'But a man could have written it.' I was confused. 'That's good then isn't it?' I asked. She sighed and said my article would be printed the following Sunday. Her sigh was explained the minute I searched through the paper. My piece was in the *Women* section. I had inadvertently been speaking to the women's editor and she had been expecting some sort of 'I felt so vulnerable on the terraces and the ever so handsome players had never met a female fan before . . .' essay. As a consequence the piece had been cut and there was no photo of me clad in my furs snuggled next to Messrs Rosenthal and Saunders.

But it was enough. I had something to show sports editors and I was given a very brief stint as a columnist in the sports pages of the *Independent on Sunday*. That led to match reports and then an intensive working week of five days on my magazine and then weekends attending football matches for whichever paper would ask me. 'I play, of course,' I would tell editor after editor. They seemed quietly impressed.

The next big breakthrough came when *The Times* wondered if I was ready to 'do a runner'. 'What's one of those?' I asked. They wanted me to try my hand at a report that went into the next day's paper, rather than one that I had the whole of Sunday morning to muse over. They gave me a match they assumed would be uneventful. It was a Cup match, Spurs v Peterborough at White Hart Lane. Spurs would win, everyone thought. And they did, but only after extra time and a penalty shoot-out. It was the biggest game of the night and it gave me, on my grown-up reportage debut, a back-page lead. Golly gosh! Actually I do not know how on earth my presence at that match was transformed, within a matter of hours of my leaving it, into a story the nation could read at their leisure.

My seat was so low in the stand all I could see were the players' knees, lots of muscular knees all as talented as each other, the lower division side's knees being if anything a shade more muscular. The Tannoy was positioned right above my head so I knew not after mis-dialling with nerves a couple of times if I had made a connection with the paper. I kept prefacing every call with the phrase 'I don't know if you can hear me, I can't hear you so I'll just talk at a slow pace and this is my first runner so don't get cross.' I dictated the progress of the penalty shoot-out directly to the chief sports sub editor and the poor chap suffered several high pitched versions of, 'And it's Anderton, he's put the ball on the spot and he's running up to the ball now and he's placed it, I can't see, oh, he's placed it to the keeper's left and it's a goal,' before he was able to communicate to me, 'Alyson, I just need to know if it's a goal or a miss.'

I am frequently asked if I feel an outsider, sat next to men in a men's world, and whether they resent my presence. Well, one or two do, I suppose, and maybe a few more just hide it very well, but that night summed it up for me. One reporter said on discovering it was my first pressure fixture that I could ask him for help if I needed it. I did not ask and he did not patronise me by offering help anyway. He was sat to my right and the chap on my left was too busy to notice if I was a woman or not. I was slightly flustered and moaned a bit about the noise but the guys just laughed, though not cruelly, and said it was usually the trickiest part of the job. One reporter took pity on the fact that my paper had time for an extra rewrite once the fireworks had finished and the crowd had dispersed and offered me some chips, and then a lift into central London. There were no sidelong glances, no cheap jibes, and to be honest I never gave and never do give the fact I might be the only female a second thought.

CHAPTER SIX

packing my boots for Euro 92

As soon as I felt faintly competent at kicking a ball, I was desperate for a game in the same way as some people are desperate for a fag. When not actually playing, I would satiate the urges by shopping for replica shirts or buying new football boots. One element of the game that marks me out as different to the men is that I have to wear the appropriate boots, football socks and shin-pads. If, on the morning of a match, I cannot find a clean pair of socks I dash to a sports shop, regardless of how busy I might be, to buy some more and, once inside the shop the pressure of work, the deadlines, the knowledge that taking an hour's break at 11 a.m. is not really acceptable, all vanish as I smooch among the Adidas and Reebok rails. In celebration of Barcelona's visit to Wembley for the European Cup final I organised tickets for my men's team and bought a Barça jacket. It was and still is beautiful, and it became a trade mark. People recognised not me but my jacket. 'You were at Wembley, weren't you?' the man in the sandwich shop said and nodded towards the woman on the till, 'My wife recognises your jacket.'

There are people who know me not as Ally but as Barça.

One of the very first football matches I reported on for a national newspaper was not the standard low-billing Watford v Walsall, but Barcelona v Real Madrid. I was so inexperienced I thought I would have to watch from a standard seat and I annoyed the sub editor on the desk in London who asked me how big the attendance was. 'How am I supposed to know that?' was my reply. I had been overawed by the whole experience. There were in fact 89,000 fans inside the Nou Camp and I had convinced the then Barcelona manager Johan Cruyff, even after he had said he wanted to retire early from the press conference because of tiredness following his major heart surgery, that he should spare me a few minutes for an interview. After that, I thought, I should retire early, and when sat in the press box at Watford one cold January evening four years later I wondered just how I had managed to start at the top and work my way down.

Too much time spent dawdling in sports shops. 'Haven't you got any red football socks, I really wanted red,' I ask the assistant.

'What size are you after?'

'They're for a teenage boy,' I reply, deciding that in football terms I am neither a male adult nor a child. They do not stock women's sizes. But when buying boots I have to come clean.

'What are you going to wear them for?' the assistant will ask.

'Oh, you know, to do the washing up in. Football, of course.'

I cannot cope with playing in the wrong sort of footwear. In the park team-mates have played in their black patent leather office shoes when they have forgotten their boots.

That I could never do. I am so close to being absolutely awful that to exacerbate the situation might, I fear, bring the world toppling in on me. At weddings when the kids are becoming bored and tearing at their waistcoats, a few sympathetic adults may start kicking a ball around with them. 'Come on Alyson, you play football don't you, get stuck in.' But I can't. Not in heels, not even in bare feet.

A recurring nightmare involves me interviewing a famous manager who, impressed by my perspicacity, invites me to join in his team's practice match. Of course they have no boots my size so they say, never mind, play in your shoes. And in shoes I look the clumsy oaf everyone expected me to be. So, it has become my prerogative to travel with boots.

Not once has this paid off. As I watched the Chelsea team training one afternoon the ball scudded to my feet. My bootless feet. My heart sank as I pulled back my leg ready to kick the ball towards Dennis Wise. I do not know how to kick a ball while wearing inappropriate footwear. So I tapped it gently and inexpertly, the way girls are expected to, while my imagination shrieked at me to flick the ball into the air and volley it into the goal.

'Hey,' called out a reporter who knew I played, 'why didn't you do something classy?'

'I wanted to, but I can't in these shoes, I mean I would have looked an idiot if I had taken my shoes off and then rummaged in my bag for my football boots, then put them on, laced them up, then warmed up – all just to give the team their ball back . . .' But he had wandered off, distracted by the far more lucid conversation offered by a pair of six-year-old autograph hunters.

I took my boots to Scandinavia. I was back-packing so I had to take just one pair, one pair that would cope with any terrain, a soggy pitch or a concrete one. I plumped for my good old reliable Astroturf boots. It was the 1992 European Championships. I had originally bought a car just for Euro 92, a slide-door non-too-sexy purple Nissan Prairie, the idea being that I could sleep in it since Scandinavia was so terribly expensive. But in the end I opted for comfort and flew.

Paradise is a tropical island with a huge deserted horse-shoe bay of white sand and sparkling turquoise water where the locals cook you dinner for under £2 and, as the sun sets, a fisherman lands with tales of lost treasure and the beautiful woman he rescued from a watery grave. No it isn't. Paradise is sitting outside a beer tent and making friends with the Danes whose nastiest insult, even when completely pissed, is to accuse a man of wearing a frilly night dress, and casting off your Englishness to become, briefly, an honorary Dane, fully accepted into their family, so you can wallow in their forthcoming victory over Germany in the Championship final.

In Scandinavia a woman alone in the middle of a football tournament is no big deal. I sat in bars and restaurants, chatted to the locals and felt completely at ease. I opted not to join the group of Russians staying in my hotel who had invited me to swim in the river at midnight. It was part of their culture, they assured me, but I was unsure why I was invited while their wives would stay to wring out the washing over the sinks in the rooms. And that was the only perturbing, remotely vulnerable moment, which ultimately was probably quite innocent.

For the first four days Sue and Paul, fellow Liverpool fans, joined me. This they did in almost parental fashion as if the idea of me wandering around northern Europe on my own for three and a half weeks was a predictably childish idea and I needed to be looked after. And I did, although not for the reasons they might have considered. Aston Villa was coming too. We stayed in Copenhagen and found a hotel with a room for four. It was remarkably good value we thought and then we saw the room. It had pull-out bunk beds. We collapsed in giggles then sprang up to fight over who would have the top bunks.

Sue and I decided we were at our sexual peak and flirted riotously in the breakfast room, on the street, on the boat to Malmö, at the matches. It was fortunate we had reached our heights in Scandinavia and not during Italia 90. In Italy we might have landed in trouble. But even the English fans in Denmark were gentlemanly.

There were two classes of England supporter. Those who had opted to be based in Copenhagen were middle-class and reasonably well educated. Those who stayed in Malmö, where England's group matches were played, were not.

We went nightclubbing and I met up with some charming Danes who had played football at school with Brian and Michael Laudrup. We talked football – and European Union politics as they were Danish, when all is said and done, and in Denmark, even if you are chatting a girl up, you need to know where she stands on the single market – until dawn and then I retraced my steps to the hotel where, upon thinking the worst, Sue sighed and said, 'Obviously my sexual peak is not quite as powerful as yours.'

Denmark had not qualified for Euro 92. They joined in only because Yugoslavia was disqualified because of its war. This was the reason Denmark won the tournament, all Scandinavia was convinced of it and knew it was the Danes' trump card right from the start. They had no time in which to become nervous or feel the pressure. It was all a bit of a laugh and how can any country, even Germany, cope with a team that is enjoying itself. The Swedish squad was just as strong as the Danes' but whenever I questioned Swedes about their team's prospects they shook their heads knowingly. 'Our team, it is good but it knows it is not good enough. It will not make the final because it knows it will not and we know it will not.'

I had a spare ticket for the Sweden v England match and offered it to every Swede I met. None took me up on the offer. Maybe there is an ancient Swedish proverb relating to avoiding English women whose biological clock is making them beam all the time, or maybe the reasons they gave were true if implausible. 'We don't really like going to matches. I'll watch it on TV. Football grounds are too uncomfortable.'

'But this is no ordinary game. This is a chance to qualify for the semi-final in your back yard. Your chance to see your country knock out a humiliated England. You must be tempted.'

'Not really, no. I have to be up early for work to-morrow.'

I could never have organised park football in Stockholm. In fact, come to think of it I never saw any park football in Stockholm. Quite how they found sufficient players to make up the national team I do not know. The Swedes summoned up more enthusiasm for English watching. They would gather to stand and watch the English supporters drinking in and around the beer tents in the same way as families gather to watch the orang-utans in the zoo. Inevitably, the shaven headed, tattooed oiks from Carlisle, Croydon and Kirkby broke free from their cages and had a tantrum. Beer bottles were smashed on the pavement, bricks were thrown through shop windows and pretty local girls with blonde plaits went home with vomit down the front of their dresses.

I travelled frequently on the ferry between Copenhagen and Malmö during my brief football sabbatical. My experience on the boat the day after the riot formed the basis of an article for the *Independent*. The Scandinavians were still polite, still helpful but their eyes misted over with reproach when they saw my Union Jack socks. I hoped the article might represent a big career break but the only stir it created revolved around a discussion in the letters pages as to why I had worn Union Jack socks to represent my Englishness and not flag of St George socks. They didn't sell St George socks in Sock Shop was the simple answer, but I dare say the grim reality of sock shopping at Heathrow Airport was not really the point of the debate.

It was during Euro 92 that I knew I somehow had to end the friendship with Aston Villa. At first I had been protective of him when Sue and Paul unleashed their sarcasm.

'You must be the best paid consultant in London.'

'Well, no not quite.'

'No, you *must* be. And the best *one* too.'

But when it came to the moment when Villa and I set off on the coach, leaving Sue and Paul at the airport, I pressed my nose against the window and mouthed at them to save me. Their broad grins said it all. It was my own fault.

Villa and I went sightseeing together. It was painful. This building reminded him of one in Tokyo, that one of one in Milan. The boats were like the boats his father sailed, the best looking women were like the ones he had shared a house with, and the only good thing about England's performance had been Aston Villa's former hero, David Platt.

I did not have the courage to say 'Go away, leave me alone.' Every time I came close he would suddenly say 'Ally, you're the only woman I've ever met who is beautiful but not vain.' Or, 'This is the best holiday I've ever had, I'm so glad we're mates.' So I was circuitous. On a tour of the nightclubs in Stockholm I said we should split up and see who could pull first. Wandering around a strange club on my own was preferable to the alternative. Occasionally I would spy Villa in the distance, trying to buy a luscious blonde a drink, and I would smile and go to the cinema for a couple of hours.

We had tickets for the Netherlands v Germany match in Gothenburg. As we stood in the railway station in Stockholm, I shrugged my shoulders and said: 'I think I'd rather watch Scotland play in Norrköping. Oh, look, there's a train to Norrköping, enjoy your match, bye.' Villa's bottom lip trembled. 'Oh come on,' I said, 'you know me and my footie, I've got to see every stadium, now, haven't I?' His lip stopped moving and he frowned, but we parted. I sat on the train and shivered with the intoxication of isolation. I was free. I put on my Russian football shirt and chatted to a Scandinavian physics professor who was curious in a cool detached scientific sort of way as to why soccer was so popular.

Norrköping, pronounced Norshopping, as in 'Are yer off t'air dressers?' 'Nor, shopping' was a miserable town that reminded me of the outskirts of Wigan. The Scots were voted best supporters of the tournament, but this was only because they held their drink better than any other fans did, never had a hope of reaching the final and found Swedish policewomen continually alluring. They were in fact the most insular fans I met and gave me the impression they were all impostors trying very hard to look like football fans when in fact they were hostile aliens assessing our gullibility. As I could not find any Russian fans (Scotland's opponents were the CIS) Norrköping was a lonely place and I trundled back to my cold hotel room to count my blessings that I was without Villa.

I was well within budget and decided after frugal Norrköping that I would indulge myself. I bought a new Sweden replica strip and had a slap-up meal in Old Stockholm. The final was in Gothenburg. I arrived late the eve before the game and visited every one-star, then two-star then three-star hotel in the city. They were all full. I turned to the four-star establishments. The first two were full but the third had a vacancy.

'Ah, in that case can I have it at a discount given it is so late and no one else will want it?'

'We do not operate a discount system in this country.'

I put on my vulnerable, pleading expression which, to be honest, does not receive much of an airing and I was not at all sure it would work. They might think I was simple. But the manager was called and after scrutinising my back-pack and my jeans somewhat surprisingly said I could have a £75 room for £40. I was very pleased with myself, bartering in Sweden was a bit less de rigueur than bartering in Turkey, but my smug smile froze when I reached my room and noticed that the waste paper bin was full, there was toothpaste in the sink, and when I turned the sheets back there were biscuit crumbs matted with pubic hair littered over the linen. I felt queasy. Was this a joke? Is this what happens in Scandinavia if you dare to knock down a price? I returned to the lobby and told the receptionist what I had found. Again the manager was summoned. And to my amazement, after he had inspected the room, he was extremely apologetic and I was given a £90 room for £40.

At breakfast the next morning the owner, a tall severe woman with her hair in a bun and an air of royalty enquired if I was quite happy. 'Ooh yes, thank you,' I said, as I munched through yet another strip of ham, feeling for all the world like the little princess in the children's stories who after years of deprivation and of rejection had found her rightful place.

None of my new Danish friends came to the final. They actually preferred to stay in Copenhagen where they could watch it on a giant screen in the town square. That way they would be with their friends and family and save money and be safe. It seemed the only Danes who were prepared physically to follow their team were the alcoholics of that race. They wobbled up and down the streets wearing Viking hats looking more like trolls than warriors. One or two leered towards me having spotted the English newspaper under my arm, but even in the midst of their beer-induced swaying they were so intelligent and courteous that I realised in that instant that English fans who beat people up are not victims of booze, they are just victims of evolution.

But still the incongruity remained. Even these Danish fans were still more interested in a discussion about which papers in the UK backed which political party than about whether Denmark could beat Germany. When Denmark did indeed beat Germany, they partied but it was a group of Brits who sang the anti-German songs and when I went in search of a bar after the match it was a British Telecom engineer from Kettering, whom I had sat next to at the France v England game, who called out to me to join him in the celebrations. I tried praising the Danish performance with some Vikings in drag but they remained modest. Even the German fans could not summon up much bile. A few joined the Danes dancing through the streets. Before the match had even finished a group of German supporters handed over a replica trophy to the Danish fans as if hopeful their team would not earn a reprieve. You lot are just too nice, we don't want to be the ones spoiling the fairy tale, they were more or less saying.

Mr BT said he and some fans from all over Europe had played a five-a-side game next to one of the stadium car parks earlier that day. I winced. I was itching to play a game and it seemed I had missed my only chance. I reflected on what might have been, the different styles of each nationality pressed together, me and the Italian sweeper nearly coming to blows, striking up a productive understanding with a Swede on the wing. I felt lonely, then, a gatecrasher on what was a Danish party, nothing to do with me.

I headed back to Copenhagen, with my football boots still wrapped in the same plastic bag, where the entire city was suffering a hang-over. The satellite link-up had been an enormous success and I had been wrong to mock it. At times like that you should be able to sweep your girl into your arms, squeeze your mother's waist and open another bottle of beer and rejoice with everyone you know, your school friends, work mates, neighbours. Part of me wished I had stayed too. Still, new friends were made and I invited anyone who was interested, to come over to London. Just one accepted the invitation and arrived six months later. He sulked when I offered to show him the sights and sat glued to the sofa watching MTV all day. As I packed my football kit together, for the Thursday night floodlit six-a-side I said he could play too if he wanted. He appeared keen but I was still surprised he dragged himself off the sofa to cross London for the game. He wore his underpants. They were boxer shorts, admittedly, but with pictures of little teddy bears printed all over them.

'What on earth are you wearing those for?' I asked him while the gang sniggered behind his back.

'I didn't know what you wear here for football and I don't like wearing jeans for it.'

Just two more days I repeated to myself, just two more days and he will be gone. Without the magic of his country's footballing exploits, he was nothing. I had fallen for the charms of his mother, his brothers, his sister, his friends, and for the grace with which Denmark had surprised European football. Never, I told myself, try to bring back part of a football experience again. It was as if I had been involved in a love affair and had thought that by baby-sitting the dream-boat's hamster I would in some way rekindle the passion.

As I dropped the hamster off at the airport I asked him why he had made the journey given that he had been intent on having as dull a time as possible. He shrugged. 'I said I would, so I did.' Yeah, I thought, you also promised to bring me a Denmark strip, but you didn't. Instead he had bought some pungent perfume at the duty free and upon presenting me with it had gone very quiet, close to tears in fact. A few hours later he had rummaged in his pockets, saying he was very short of cash and then produced the duty free receipt. Look how much I spent at the airport, he said. I gave the receipt a quick glance and grunted disinterestedly.

Dismayed he edged closer. 'Look, that is for my cigarettes and that, that there, is for your perfume.'

'Shall I pay you for it then?'

'No, of course not,' he said, 'but if you could buy in some more beers . . .'

Some Viking.

I left my boots at home when I went to Madrid. When young, supple, gorgeous and 17 my friend Caroline and I had vowed that should we ever reach the age of 30 – Caroline believed she would, in all probability have committed suicide by then – we would commiserate by visiting a city neither of us had at that point been to. Caroline does not like football and to take my boots would have been disloyal and pointless. We settled on Madrid. It had the reputation of having a vibrant clubbing scene and offering sophisticated lunches, together with decent architecture and atmosphere. Silently I noted that I had never entered either of its two famous football stadiums.

An hour after our plane had landed we were comfortably settled in our chairs out on the pavement of a pretty square, the autumn sunshine casting flattering shadows over us in best frocks and hats as we supped Cava. We toasted this and that, received the gift of flowers from admirers with polite aloofness but was there a slight frown crinkling my forehead? Yes, yes there was, and Caroline noticed it.

'So, which football match are we going to see then?' she asked.

'Oh, no we couldn't go to a game, this is your weekend too. It's our girls' time-out, I see football all the time, I can live without it for one weekend.'

'It's all right,' she said soothingly. 'I fully expected to go to a match and I have prepared myself for it. In fact I'm almost looking forward to it.'

The frown disappeared as I leapt up to investigate the availability of tickets. Real Madrid were away in Tenerife but Atletico Madrid were at home to, joy of joys, Barcelona. I informed Caroline of how lucky we were.

She said she would have to take my word for it.

As we approached the stadium the enormity of the occasion finally hit Caroline. There were armed police on horses down every nook and cranny and minor scuffles breaking out with the alacrity of corn popping in a microwave. She held on tightly to my arm. 'Is this normal?' she asked.

The Vicente Calderón stadium did not disappoint. It was just like a cauldron with fanaticism bubbling away all around the ground. Barcelona took a 3–0 lead in at half-time. The man sat to my left started groaning and rocking to and fro in his seat. He had travelled all the way from Guatemala to see his beloved Atletico and he was in despair.

'It'll be OK,' I told him.

'Will it? Really? How will it?'

Summoning my most authoritative voice I proceeded to guarantee him that Atletico would score at least three times in the second half. 'I have seen a lot of Barça recently,' I told him, 'and they will crumble over the next 45 minutes. They look too confident and Atletico will rip into them. I'm right, just wait.' I was more right than I knew. The home side scored three goals and then won the match with a fourth.

'You are wonderful,' said the Guatemalan after the third

goal had gone in. When the fourth was scored he fell to his knees. 'You are the Madonna,' he sobbed.

'Oooh, I'm very impressed.' said Caroline. 'Does this happen to you every time you go to a match?'

Regrettably, it does not.

CHAPTER SEVEN

rituals

The park footballer's natural enemy is softball. This is a cross between rounders and baseball and in Regent's Park is played as a form of corporate entertainment. The main reason it incurs our wrath and spoils our game is that it takes up so much park space on sunny days, days when space is at a premium. And the softball game stretches past its immediate boundary as a good hit means one of the participants runs blindly onto the football pitch their eyes raised heavenwards as they follow the path of the usually not so soft ball.

More irritating still are the people involved. They are usually an unappetising mixture of enthusiastic Americans, unathletic British gents and giggling office girls. They wear matching baseball caps and T-shirts with corporate logos and bring baskets of drink and food. They are to sport what poodles are to dog racing.

More annoying still is the fact that English law gives them more of a right to play in Regent's Park than we have. I know this because I have been threatened with arrest after disputing it. Early in the Regent's Park season, just after the start of British Summer Time, police cars roam the territory in much the same way as safari trucks roam through the jungle spying on wildlife. Sometimes the police just watch and then leave, sometimes they tell us to stop playing football.

The first time this happened we were so astounded that we did not argue, we just waited for the police to move on and then we started up our game again. This was the tactic employed by all the other teams in the park and it was quite a sight, a dozen separate huddles of men suddenly standing still, scuffing at the turf as if waiting for a lift or in a queue for the cinema, and then slowly, one by one, each huddle would spring into life as the police moved farther away.

On the next occasion that the police told us to pack it in, I asked them why we should. A young but weary officer said we were damaging the grass and that the area of park we were in had been set aside for hockey matches.

'Hockey damages the grass, too,' I said. 'In fact it is worse for it; hockey players dig the turf up with their sticks.'

'I am not getting into a discussion, you cannot play football here.'

'But it is our right. Football is part of the English heritage. You've let the softball carry on and that is American.'

At this point both policemen looked angry but just as I expected my team-mates to steal in with a clever comment to back me up, one of them laughed nervously and said of course we would move. And the legal big-wig of our gang had mysteriously vanished. I had spoken out secure in the knowledge that he was standing behind me filled with the same indignation but with more insight into our rights. But when I turned round he had disappeared into the trees.

'Tom, Tom, where did you go? We needed you.' Tom said, avoiding eye contact, that in his high-profile job, he could not afford a scrap with the police. Wimps. Wimps the lot of you, I thought and I vowed to take the matter up with my MP, the Football Association and the Parks Commission, but I never did because football survives even in the strictest police state. We never lost more than ten minutes of play as a consequence of this police intransigence. Twice we had to leave our section of the park and cross Chester Road, nearer to the Open Air Theatre, and play there instead. This is designated soccer land and far less romantic as a consequence. It is a snooty version of Hackney Marshes. The land is flat and there are no trees. The myriad games were all set up at right angles to each other and it was hard to tell where one match's parameters began and another one's ended. In our favoured bit of Regent's Park, near Ulster Terrace, the ground undulates and trees are scattered everywhere. We have played on square, rectangular, hexagonal and diamond shaped pitches when needs must. The boys can sidle over to the woodland when they need to relieve themselves and when the sun sets, the wedding cake houses on the Outer Circle turn from icing sugar white to deep luxurious orange. And when the sun has dipped out of sight we play a little while longer by the light of British Telecom Tower.

We have often been the last to leave the park, and if we owned a luminous ball we would stay longer still. By the time the light has dimmed the game has altered. We are fewer in number and half of those left are moaning that they cannot see anything. Once, Orrin, who is black, wore a white T-shirt and looked like a headless corpse. Once this was pointed out we all giggled every time he had the ball. Giggling is not part of park football but when you are playing in the dark the rules change. When we are playing blindman's boot it generally means I have lost control. I am usually the one who calls out that 'Next goal wins'. I never do this on a whim. I do it when more than one player has expressed the opinion that the game has run out of steam and I agree with them. But when we play in the dark, that means there has been a kind of mutiny and someone else keeps shouting that we will play for another five minutes, and then another and another.

Once I left my glasses behind and three of us returned as the pubs closed. We scaled the gates and found our favoured piece of England's soil a dark and scary place. We hiccuped our way to where we had played and tried a kick about in a darkness which was all the darker for being sudden and not one that had gradually enveloped us. We could not find my glasses and then we lost the ball.

All that groping in the dark is a feature of early autumn, when our time out in the park is cruelly limited. In those first years it also presaged the doom of a winter without any football at all. What we had to do was find a way to play all year round. That, given we are a nation devoted to soccer, proved surprisingly difficult. I phoned around various floodlit pitches in central London and was told that the waiting lists were five years long. I put our name down all the same and I still have not heard from them.

Finally we found the Westbourne Green Sports Complex, just west of Paddington. For many of us it was inconveniently situated and meant a two-hour journey home, but for seven years it has represented our soccer alter-ego. Now, when a chill pervades the air and the light dims, Carl starts yearning for Westbourne Green, and when the blossom bursts Sean starts yearning for the park.

Carl prefers the rigidity of our winter home. The pitches vary a bit in size and design and we have played on most of them, but they all have walled boundaries, real nets and require rules; no shooting from inside the semi-circle, the ball must be kept below head height. The accent is on close control, quick passing and accurate finishing and the harder you work, the more you get out of it. For Carl, park football is too free-form. The ball can be booted 100 yards to the left or right and then chased by two players who lunge at each other, two comic figures in the distance trying to win a private battle, while the rest of you stand around waiting for them to rejoin the game. Goals are disputed on a regular basis and without the benefit of goalposts we adopt the maxim, when in doubt, rule it out, so the score at the end is often 8–9 if you count Ally's dubious volley, 7–9 if you don't, or 8½–9½ for times when we cannot agree. If you like life to be ordered, it can be frustrating. But then, for Sean, the enclosed pitches enclose his mind, and make him feel like a caged animal. Sean loves to slide tackle and on the concrete that brings no reward; on the grass it makes him look like Denis Irwin. Both Carl and Sean agree that both forms of football are better than none, however, and both, I am pleased to report, have an excellent attendance record.

Our winter game is fraught with complications and attendance is one of the biggest. The quality of Westbourne stragglers is poor, so if our numbers dip we are forced to play against lippy eight-year-olds. They are not all-weather pitches either, although that usually does not deter us. One particularly cold winter I borrowed a tub of Saxa cooking salt from the staff kitchen and spent 20 fairly pointless minutes pouring it over the patches of ice that threatened to turn our game into a limb massacre. We have played paddle football after a downpour that left us ankle deep in water I could not shift with the broom. Fallen leaves mean we skid dangerously into the walls.

Our cheap leather balls lose their covering within minutes and our knees become raw. When I last fell at Westbourne it was shortly after I had recovered from a broken arm and in the split second available to make any choice in these matters I decided to take the brunt of the impact on my face, not wishing to break my arm again. I was rewarded with a scraped, bleeding chin and a piece of gravel lodged in my lip giving the impression, which lasted for several weeks, that I had, in a spurt of vanity, had a collagen implant. Overall, I was quite pleased with the result.

But of all the drawbacks, the worst is losing the ball. We play most of our games on pitches that back onto a large dimly lit car-park for a block of flats. All it takes is one mis-timed shot for the ball to zoom over the fence and the game to be held up. The guilty party, unless it is Tom as he is over 50, or me, as I am suddenly a helpless female, has to run around the whole complex to reach the car-park and then crawl around between the cars and the bins looking for the ball. It used to be that every time the ball was kicked over we would all groan and shake our heads at whoever was responsible, but now we cheer and shout 'Go on Lawrence'. Lawrence is a new regular and bravely scales the wall and fence thus cutting out the ten-minute trip around all the pitches. Lawrence's build and attitude and style all suit the park much better and it takes him half of every game to adapt to the six-a-side pitch, thus switching from liability to match-winner disconcertingly quickly. This is not behaviour many of my moaning and deeply conservative minnies can stomach but Lawrence's ball-retrieving skills have already secured his position in legend.

Five years ago I was desperate to move out of my Docklands flat where my cat had to be kept hidden from the landlord and any sense of vibrancy had to be kept hidden from the region's inhabitants. I decided I had to live right slap bang in the middle of the best London could offer but discovered that letting-agents specialise in letting prospective clients know just how pathetic a desire that is on an average income.

The ubiquitous Greg recommended an agent he had used and found to be non-judgemental. I called her on that basis alone without asking what area of London she covered. She showed me a horrid studio room in Kensington and then, just a little irritated by my unwillingness to sign away a year's salary on the first place I had seen, she took me to a flat in Bayswater. The omens were overpowering. On the way to the flat it emerged she was married to the brother of a girl I had gone to school with in Lancashire, and as I studied the A-Z I realised this flat was only a ten-minute walk away from the flat of my new boyfriend. But the clincher was the realisation that courtesy of a well-hidden alley, the flat was also only five minutes walk away from the Westbourne Green Sports Complex and our six-a-side pitches. I happily signed away a year's salary on only the second place I had viewed and never regretted it. I could change into my kit in the comfort of my own home, sat next to my out-in-the-open cat, skip to football, skip to the pub afterwards, skip to the supermarket for rump steaks, and then skip home for a long bath having enticed the new love in my life to join me for the remainder of the evening. What a thoroughly perfect existence.

Or it would have been and would be if I could just look at my watch and think 'time I set off for football' and then leave. But, for a 6 p.m. kick-off in the park, I start thinking about my preparations at 2 p.m. That is 2 p.m. the previous day. I have evolved a routine that is obsessive, pathetic and painful. At 2 p.m. the previous day I wonder if my socks and shorts need washing and, if they do, I wash them. I then consider dinner. I prefer simpler meals with a low alcohol accompaniment the evening before a match. On the day of a game I drink plenty of water and eat pasta for lunch whether I want it or not. Gnocchi with butter and grated parmesan is my preferred option and when I yearn for a cup of tea afterwards I shake my head and reach for the Volvic or Highland Spring instead. At around 4 p.m. I start hunting for my sports bra. This takes about an hour even though it is always on the floor of the airing cupboard and I only look there as a last and desperate resort. I then empty my sports bag of rubbish and pack my boots. I lay out my socks, shorts and chosen replica football shirt before driving to pick up my son from his nursery. His baby-sitter turns up at 5 p.m. and smiles weakly as I turn the cupboard under the stairs inside out searching for my shin-pads. 'I can't bloody find my shin-pads,' I tell her. This happens every week and is sometimes supplemented by me telling her that I can't find my bloody hair band. I then put on my football gear and jog to the bus stop. I am 50 yards down the road when I turn back because I have forgotten to put the shin-pads in my bag.

After the bus I take the tube, always stopping at the same kiosk to buy an over-priced designer sports drink. I sit on the tube and stare at my watch wondering wildly why it is all such a breathless dash when I have tried to be organised.

I try to read the paper but find myself deliberating what sort of mood I am in. Unless I am happy with the world I will not play too well.

I always use the loo at the same pub near Regent's Park and always marvel at the beauty of the park as I walk to where we will play. I hate being late and rarely am in spite of the rigmarole of my preparation. I issue sarcastic rebukes to latecomers whose own sarcastic rebukes should I be late are not acknowledged. I then exchange a lament with Kier that we are both paying very expensive baby-sitters for the privilege of being there, put on my head band and start to warm up. After performing a series of silly stretches I then also tie my hair back, assuming I have remembered the extra hair band. And so after 28 hours of flapping, fidgeting and worrying I am ready to start flapping, fidgeting and worrying about who is on my team and who is missing. Throughout the game I readjust the 'goalposts', ruminate over the wind direction, the glare of the setting sun and the arrogance of a newcomer who is not half as talented as he thinks he is. He, no doubt, is wondering who that little old woman is and why is she playing and then I take the ball off him and all of it, all the hassle, all the organisation, is worthwhile.

CHAPTER EIGHT

replica life

Every week we play and every week we are on different sides. The teams are chosen on the basis of uniformity of shirt colour rather than balance of skills. When I was at the peak of my fits of pique, when I strove to make the games as near to real football as I possibly could, I would despair at how varied the shirts were and dread an uneven number of participants. If I was late or distracted and the boys themselves had settled on two sides I would cast my eyes over their shoddy workmanship in despair.

'No that will not work. Look at Steve. His shirt's practically identical to Andy's. How can they be on opposite sides?' And so the game's start would be delayed as I set about rectifying the errors. I am slightly less dictatorial now but there still has to be order. It can be Whites v Colours, or Bright v Dull, or Stripes v The Rest, or Replica Strips v Lack of Imagination. I have made grown men play in bad weather without any shirt at all if my system requires it.

Every week there is a shirt that is unclassifiable. Every week for the past ten years that shirt has been worn by one man and it has never occurred to Kier to wear another one. As the years have passed the shirt has moved from being a honorary striped one, to a colourful one, to a dull one and has now faded into a white one. When all else fails we have played the 'plus system' of for example Whites v Colours plus Kier.

The annoyance I have experienced upon dividing the group into two easily definable teams of Dark v Light only for a latecomer to turn up wearing a black and white Newcastle strip is so deeply felt that I probably qualify for NHS obsessive/compulsive behaviour therapy. We almost tried bibs once, but park football and bibs do not mix. Your team immediately looks pretentious and soft. I find bibs emasculating, and I am not a man, so I can quite understand any man who says he does not want to wear one. Professional teams wear them in training and during practice matches of course but in the park you are not training, you are not practising, you are playing, so it is forbidden to wear them.

So, every week the sides are different and every week there is an instant camaraderie struck up between those whom fate has thrown together. It matters for those 90 minutes or so whether we can beat the other side, most of whom might have been playing alongside us the week before. And at the end we assess why we won or why we should have, briefly excluding the opposition.

One glorious summer's evening as the real England team prepared for the World Cup finals by participating in the Tournoi de France so many of us turned up for Regent's Park football that we decided to hold our own Tournoi de Regent's Parc. Never before had we attracted so many play- ers that we could not contain them within a single match. I pranced around organising everyone singing, 'We're having a tournoi, we're having a tournoi' and it was such splendid fun. I was in charge of time-keeping, 25 minutes per match, which I abused slightly if my side were trailing and which might have been the reason why we won. Just by injecting a slightly more competitive spirit the atmosphere altered. It was more festive and more heartfelt. The strength of the instant camaraderie intensified and we all tried that little bit harder, pushed ourselves further. One team was vilified for being a push-over, another for being dirty, and another for playing beautiful football without being able to score. We are all one, but once again we were separated by the concept of the team.

Sometimes it is a mass influx of new players that twangs at the camaraderie heart strings. Obviously we do not let too many strangers in at once, but just now and again a group of guys, known to maybe one or two of us decides to give park football a go. Because they know some of us they feel comfortable and at home, so at home that they can start a row almost immediately with another player who riles them. One summer, in about Year Seven, four friends and a friend of a friend of Adrian's turned up. Dunc wore glasses, took them off and proceeded to squint menacingly with every unadventurous pass. Mike, thin, pale, even sickly looking, was far too good. He stopped half way through for a smoke and our team disintegrated for as long as it took his left lung to discuss the irony of the situation with his right lung. He would dribble, sometimes gratuitously, always effortlessly, score a beautifully economical goal and not even twitch his eyebrows. There was much muttering that he was not of our ilk.

And there was Terry. Terry was almost professionally Geordie. Naturally he wore a Newcastle shirt, but he seemed to hate Sunderland more than he loved Newcastle. He arrived slightly cocky, slightly mistrustful and rather than engage in conversation, which would have been odd anyhow, he threw comments at the other players. He assumed we would all share his perceptions of the world, his prejudices and his humour. But when he accused our goalkeeper of wearing socks that were too clean, Old Fogey Peter, who takes keeping most seriously, took offence. Bad move. Terry pushed the point. 'What are yer, gay or sommat?'

Unfortunately Peter bristled and appeared more camp than he ever had before. 'That Terry, he ploughs his own furrow doesn't he?' he said later. Terry overheard and was mightily amused, so amused that whenever one of his passes went astray he would snigger, 'Here I go again, ploughing my own furrow. Hey, what the bloody hell does that mean anyhows?' Terry wound up quite a few of our regulars but I liked playing with him. We had a strange telepathy and every single one of his goals was set up by me. Perhaps it had something to do with the way his shorts never made it as high as his waist and by the time he had taken his hat-trick would be closer to his knees than his buttocks. 'Pull your shorts up,' someone would shout, but Terry refused even to try. He never ran and when he could, he stood still. Tackling, he said, was too much like hard work. The regulars were not exactly depressed when he stopped coming.

The park is a barometer for the status of football. Football is a bandwagon. Those who never think about it suddenly found themselves glued to the telly when we met Germany in the semi-final of Euro 96, and of course the park was packed, too. Inspired by a surge of soccer nationalism, thousands of men rummaged in their cupboards for the football boots they last wore at college and headed for the park with their mates. They inevitably sprain an ankle or pull a hamstring – patriotism does not stretch to sensible warm-up exercises. Indeed after one of my crusades to force the men at my office to join the movement I was indirectly responsible for a glut of absenteeism as one unfit executive after another fell foul of the scorched-earth policy of park life.

The higher up the executive ladder the bigger the label on their brand new sports shirt. One boss bought brand new everything, which was a big mistake as the rest of us just could not resist wading in with the dirty tackle. He was as tempting to kick as it must be for a kid to pinch a fat, dribbling, mollycoddled toddler, as he preened nervously and criticised the way the ball had bobbled just before he had struck it.

Ten summers of playing football in the park has taught me some invaluable sociological and anthropological lessons. The park is not just my arena for fantasy, it is everyone's. The unwritten rules, as fixed as if we had a formal consti- tution, that govern our society state that if you wear a replica football shirt anywhere other than inside a football stadium or in the park, then you are an unfashionable git, probably on the dole. But we all want to wear the kit, wear it all the time, so given the excuse, footie in the park, we go crazy.

I used to be the one who went craziest of them all. There was one summer when it seemed important I wore a different shirt every week, as if knowing I lacked flair in my play I could make up for it by inducing cries of 'Ally, Italy away kit, very nice.' Or 'Ally, whose shirt is that? It looks familiar though. Ah Benfica, very nice.' There are three reasons why I have stopped buying new shirts. The first is age. I no longer look faintly cute in any old thing. To be honest, these days I look haggard in my yellow Sweden strip. You have to be young and tanned to get away with bright yellow nylon with bold blue stripes on an ungainly V-neck. And I feel a little more, well, mature and sensible. These replica kits cost a lot of money and I have been buying them for so long now that the older ones have near-classic status so I can start wearing them again if I feel the need to impress.

The second reason is envy. I was being out-performed by Frank. Frank is too good a player to need gimmicks so the overall effect just beat mine hands down. Frank's speciality is Newcastle shirts. I had no idea the club issued so many different designs but as soon as a new one is released, Frank has it, and often has it first because he has 'connections'. Frank seemed to abide by my rules. That is, you can wear any shirt you like, but you must be loyal to the English club you support. So he can wear a Celtic shirt for example or a Chile strip but not one representing another English club. Then one afternoon Frank arrived wearing an Oldham shirt. It was brand new, out later that week, full of novelty value, but Frank had made a big mistake. When it came to our Christmas awards dinner I dismayed everyone by making it obvious I harboured a petty grudge by not giving Frank the Devotion to Replica Kit Award. No one else even remembered Frank wearing an Oldham shirt and if they had they would probably have remembered his apologetic excuse, 'I forgot my Newcastle shirt and some guy in the office had just been involved in arranging Oldham's sponsorship so he gave me this.' But, oh no, that was not good enough for puritanical Ally and poor Frank did not receive the trophy he deserved.

The third reason is that I now own the ultimate shirt

and do not really enjoy wearing anything else. It is a lovely rosy-red long-sleeved Liverpool shirt modelled on the 1965 strip they wore for the FA Cup final that year. It has white cuffs and round white collar and a simple embroidered Liverbird crest. It is made of thick cotton and far too warm for 96 per cent of the year, but I sweat happily away because it guarantees me a goal before I have even warmed up. By contrast the shiny, complicated, sponsor-driven shirts of today are tacky in the extreme and become dated after only six months. The nastiest thing on a park pitch is Liverpool's shirt from last season, it grates on the nerves because something is obviously not quite right, the detail jars, and the most beautiful thing on a park pitch is a shirt three decades old. Class, it shrieks, class.

Liverpool shirts, even in London's Regent's Park, are the most popular of all. This is a comment on employment, or lack of it, in the north-west, a comment on the pride Liverpool supporters feel for the club, and it backs up surveys which state that more Liverpool fans are to be found living away from the environs of Anfield than any other fans are to be found living at a distance from their team. It is also a sign that Liverpool are a big club, with a large support base, yet I rarely see a Manchester United strip. This settles once and for all the debate that rages over whether Man United have real supporters. Clearly their solid support is still in Manchester and those hangers-on who have never been north of Enfield, let alone lived in Manchester, who claim to be part of Alex Ferguson's all-conquering army, do not feel sufficiently enamoured with the team to bother wearing its strip. They would be too embarrassed to. It is one thing being able to trot out over a pint that you support the Reds but quite another to plaster it unconvincingly over your torso. On the other hand they may all be just too weary of the jibes and threats of violence. Everyone hates Man United so why invite reprisals?

South American shirts are very popular in Regent's Park. If a bloke is wearing an Argentina or Brazil shirt, is short and olive-skinned you know, before he has kicked a ball, he will be tremendously skilful and selfish. If, however, he is wearing a Belgrano Athletic top, is tall, skinny and fair skinned, he will be talentless, arrogant and selfish. Two men wearing the same shirt asking to join your match are to be avoided; they will only pass to each other, especially if they both have long hair.

Replica shirts are part of the fun of the park until they are taken too seriously. It is strictly infra dig to wear matching replica shorts once past 12 years of age. I once wore matching shorts because I could see no other occasion on which I might give them an airing, splendid birthday gift that they were, and I was completely mortified. Overdoing the replica is like overdoing the hair-spray, or overdoing the varieties of sherry you offer guests before dinner, or overdoing the ingratiation of the boss so you end up taking his triplets to Butlins on your week off. It is nice to have a rest from replica now and again, and if you have over-indulged, then a plain white baggy T-shirt is as refreshing as iced tea in the midday sun after a fortnight of retsina and extra sticky baklavas.

I can spot the guys who are comfortable with the skills they possess, they have simply grabbed the nearest shirt on their way out of the house; the ultimate laid-back blokes are simply wearing the shirt that has lain stewing in perspiration at the bottom of the bag from the week before. Some men are afraid to make a statement of any kind and opt for the shirt that is grey and insipid so no one can accuse them of being flash. Perhaps they would like to move up a gear and wear a daringly plain blue T-shirt but I make it difficult. 'Oooh, Nigel, you must want to be on my side this week, you don't normally wear that shirt do you.'

Overall, the plainer the top, the better the player. The razzmatazz of replica is often a substitute for natural ability or an indication of vanity or insecurity, neither of which is fun to line up with. Only when you know the players well can you discern those who go replica for parody or for a joke. It is perfectly possible to be a replica and to be a first rate park player, but it may take many years of analysis before the truth of it can be gauged.

Few sights are more pitiful than the corporate soccer team, however. I have been part of many and none has been a personal success. The format is for a large employer to organise a five-a-side tournament that will engender company camaraderie and impress clients. They take place on indoor wooden or felt pitches ringed by a viewers' gallery and close to a subsidised bar. The participants steadily drink pint of lager after pint of lager, interrupting their merriment only to play five or ten minutes of football. Some teams wear specially printed T-shirts with the company's logo on it. Some teams wear matching T-shirts with a sad slogan that bears no relation to their employer but were left over from a fun run one of their mothers ran in seven years ago. I played several times for my old magazine and we must have looked the saddest of all for we had bought a real kit and paid for our company logo to be sewn on to it, but we were still pretty awful footballers.

I used to become quite excited by these tournaments. Anything with a trophy at the end of it made my eyes glisten like a magpie's. Invariably they proved disappointing. None of the teams was interested in playing decent football. They wanted to win, and look hard and break someone's leg as they did it. Cramped onto the tiny courts, penned in by concrete walls, there was little I could do to make any impact. I hated the ball, which was made either of plastic or the stuff they make tennis balls out of, and most of all I hated the air. There was not enough of it. The courts had an intense dryness that added to the sensation that this was combat, not football. There were constant collisions and that nice boy in design would suddenly be transformed into a snarling, rabid animal as he sought out retribution for a late tackle.

All the other women were wives and girlfriends and they sat in the bar reading the Sunday papers, occasionally asking how it was going and smiling at my bruised knees while saying how brave I was to participate. Some dragged themselves to the viewing gallery to cheer on their team and the standard practice was to cheer whenever I, as the token woman, touched the ball regardless of what I did with it. I would have handled all this very well had I played a blinder or scored the winning goal, but I never did. I would manage one decent pass per ten-minute match before being pushed to the hard floor or pinned against the concrete wall by a large, sweating, unfit, but highly competitive, sales director. It was so competitive that no one ever questioned the presence of a woman. The other teams just thought it meant their chances of victory were improved by my team's folly.

My last ever indoor tournament, at least I have vowed it will be my last, was the most patronising of them all. The competition's rules stated that each team had to include one woman who had to play at least five minutes of each ten-minute match. Greg asked me to play for his office team. 'Aren't there any women in your company who want to play?' I asked. 'Nooo' he wailed and so, in spite of the fact it was on a Friday evening and I would have to leave my small son with a perfect stranger, I agreed.

As I feared, none of the other token women had played football before and they giggled mercilessly as they waited to enter the arena for their five minutes. Women who have never played before have a certain gait. Their feet are splayed and they lean backwards as they approach the ball. They kick at the ball as if it is a dirty rag in their path, and if they are enthusiastic they chase around the pitch with enormous, smiling gusto. They are totally unpredictable; one even managed to score when her mis-kick completely fooled the keeper. She squeaked and ran around in circles, and her friends from the office squeaked too. It was like being surrounded by over-sized pissed mice. I did not like what I saw because it reminded me of my first ever matches, when I must have looked the same and now I hoped I looked the part but feared that I did not.

My team, all strangers bar Greg, thanked me for being there but it was gratitude borne of being female and prepared to help them out, not the gratitude for a game well played. I sullenly explained my footballing pedigree over a pint after we had been knocked out and having registered their amazement that I had not only played before but for ten years, I wandered out alone, desperate for some nice polluted London air. It is very, very difficult to become one of the Heroes of Football.

CHAPTER NINE

the manageress has blood on her hands

Channel 4 screened a series a good few years ago now called *The Manageress*. It starred Cherie Lunghi as a woman taking charge of a professional football team and was a programme I watched with morbid fascination.

It was actually very good in terms of the acting and getting the feel of a team right. The banter between players was convincing and many of the subplots were funny and fairly believable. But the basic theme, that a woman could be a league football manager, was none of these things. I took it too seriously, of course. It was meant to be a crazy notion but that, for me, was the problem. I did not consider it to be a crazy notion. I objected instead to it becoming crazy by virtue of the circumstances of Ms Lunghi's background.

She had never played football. She was a bloody aerobics teacher with a posh voice and a fur coat whose father gave a football club sufficient money to buy her the job as the string attached. She excelled in scenes where she redesigned the team's strip, but the very idea anyone would take a blind bit of notice about her views on tactics was ludicrous. After all, just making sure my phone calls are returned when I am trying to organise a match is difficult enough – and I am a player/manager, not some honey-voiced groupie who likes watching Italian football because the men are so tanned and look after their bodies better than their English counterparts.

The managerial difficulties I face are not entirely rooted in my gender. In every group there is an organiser, a proportion happy to be organised, a proportion who are not, and the remainder who have no view, but simply float through life wanted or unwanted and care not either way. When I offered to be the lead juror in court, my fellow jurors fell into the usual pattern and I had a bit of trouble with a couple of middle-aged housewives who thought I was too big for my boots. I was not and I know this because sometimes I can be. What they objected to was being directed. They wanted a good gossip about the case and I, in the interests of justice, would not let them.

Of course the pay-off for me, in football, is that I get to play. If another player had organised the games, the real games, not the haphazard park games, I might have been permanently glued to the subs' bench or perhaps conveniently overlooked. More likely the games would never have happened. And I am so insecure about my ability that I rarely play for the full 90 minutes with the guys – so much for the perk of being the boss.

But I am not the boss, not really.

Having painstakingly ensured we have 11 players and a sub or two, I set about slotting them into place on the pitch. During boring meetings, or over a pint, I sketch formations. There are players whose position is obvious and secure. Ed, for example, was a superb flame-haired

Scottish centre forward before his job took him too far away to ever make a kick-off on time. Ed loves Man United and had developed the body language of Denis Law. Ed could be there on the basis of his talent, personality and his reasonable attendance.

But those who turn up to the park every week and are less personable and less talented still have to be asked if they want to join the special 11-a-side match, too. In many respects professional managers have it easy. They are beholden to no one and if they decide a striker should be in defence, then the striker either obliges or he goes on the transfer list. Now and again, when a manager is a nice sort you sense that the players may have more control than is healthy, but I doubt Roy Evans will appreciate this pathetic attempt to draw a parallel with his man-management and mine.

I once, after dozens of attempts, finalised my team-sheet. It was easy to show it to Ed, for example, but less easy to show it to a player who saw himself as a midfield maestro and I had pushed him into 'right-back, coming on in the second half'. Here the real managers took over. I might exert slight authority over the relatively new gang members but I have no special credentials in the eyes of those who were founder members of our park team and they swiftly rearranged my meticulous design. They did this without fuss and without anger but with the aplomb of a parent correcting basic algebra in their precocious ten-year-old's homework. There are some things dads know best, and some things men know best.

When we are losing, I always bring myself off. I do not have the gall to pull off one of the men and, in any case, my belief that I, as the woman, am the weak link in a game being contested between men is hardly far-fetched. But recently I was not the player/manager, I was just the plain old boss, the guv'nor, chief, the manager. Lawrence, one of the more recent additions to our band of merry men, and as a consequence more susceptible to my act of being in complete control of them, asked if I would arrange a game between Ally's team and his work-mates. I agreed and then promptly broke my foot.

I would like very much to describe the manner of my powerful run into the penalty area, how I leapt like a springbok to head the ball into the back of the net while the keeper arched his back but just could not reach and as I landed a stocky defender made a late challenge which meant I fell awkwardly and snapped my left foot. I would like that very much but instead I have to relate that I was at home and had glanced at the clock, seen it was later than I thought and been about to dash out when I remembered I had a complaint about my dry cleaning. There was a crease in a shirt and it was annoying me. Such girlie thoughts deserved punishment and sure enough as I hurtled down the stairs carrying my shirt in one hand and my other laundry in the other I slipped and misjudging how near the bottom I was because my view was obscured by the damnable creased shirt I landed on my foot with it pointing vertically downwards. I heard it snap and my first thought was, 'Oh no my football.' I hollered a very unattractive word a couple of dozen times over, growled for a while, and then crawled to the phone.

But I had said I would organise the game for Lawrence, so I did. I was absurdly flattered that even in my new-found more relaxed approach to football nights, I am still regarded as the prime organiser, the leader, the one who gets things done. It had been a while since I had attempted to organise the boys for a proper match, but a bunch of social workers described as 'all right, not that good really', sounded ideal fodder.

I abandoned my bullying tactics and instead decided I would adopt a spiral approach, asking all the most loyal team members first whether they could or wanted to play. With my leg in plaster I arranged everything by fax or phone. It was exasperating. Dave sounded keen and was definite that he could make it but the others reacted as if I was cold-calling them about a double-glazing offer.

'Well, when is it? Oh. Well I'm not sure really. Yeah, I think so, probably. I've just remembered I think we've got people over. I'll have to check.'

I ploughed on regardless. I did not lose my temper, I did not question their commitment to the cause. Finally with the bare bones of a team in place I stopped phoning but I worried whether anyone would remember to turn up. And then, like that scene at the end of *It's a Wonderful Life*, just when I despaired of my team-mates exhibiting any enthusiasm, and with five days to go before kick-off, they jammed my switchboard.

'Ally, sorry, Ally-boss, it's still on isn't it? Do you want me to bring shirts for everyone.'

'Ally, I mean Guv'nor, do you need a keeper?'

'Ally, um, Mrs Manager, what position am I playing?'

I thought I could detect real concern. One or two were actually worried about whether they were seen as first-choice players and what position they would be forced to adopt. After a lengthy preamble in which topics we would never normally discuss were raised and

I discovered that a literature bore, a divorce bore and a Jazz FM bore lay behind the footballing façade of several of my team-mates, the big question would be asked. 'So, Ally, where exactly were you thinking of me playing then, not that I mind obviously, I just wondered, you know.'

Mums, wives, girlfriends and offspring turned up to cheer us on, or perhaps more pertinently to catch a glimpse of the man in their lives they frequently berated for being a fat, no-good layabout behaving athletically. If they had hoped to see their men transformed into Adonis or Hercules they were disappointed for the strip we had borrowed was none too flattering and its nasty, tight acrylic texture accentuated every wedge of flab. The advantage in women's football I reflected was that the strips handed down to us by men's teams were inevitably too large for us so that even the plumpest gal could hide her rippled parts. Far better to do what the opposition were doing and wear more or less matching T-shirts. In their case it meant their skinniness was disguised but the overall effect was one of laid-back toughness.

The opposition were all social workers, men forced to be pleasant to 40-a-day pregnant women with husbands who liked to make sure the bath water is always scalding hot, so we should have known it was bound to be a dirty match. Frank went to hospital after 25 minutes with a head wound. He had bravely dived in to score and emerged with blood oozing over his face and cascading down his shirt. Unfortunately we did not have any spare shirts so his replacement had to put on Frank's. It was drenched in blood, heavy and wet with gore and it clung to the substitute's skin. And to think I had doubted my team's commitment. I wondered if I had been fit to play and on the subs' bench whether I would have pulled on Frank's damp DNA-matted number 8 jersey. I think I probably would.

The number 10 shirt had lain overlooked by them all, a general unwillingness to be seen to think themselves worthy of the shirt that heralds the play-maker and the star, having overtaken them. I, on the other hand, would have grabbed it the minute the kit bag was dropped to the floor and as I felt my muscles twitching as I watched them huff and puff up and down the pitch, I knew I would have done anything, even bathed in another's blood, to have been part of it.

At the same time that Frank collapsed, Dave suffered a dead leg, and so Gary, who should have been on from the start but was late, replaced him. There was a surreal symmetry to all this. Gary had only just finished tying his laces and Richard, Frank's replacement, had turned up unexpectedly just in case he was needed. It had bothered me that we had too many players. I did not want to pull anyone off and was deciding who would have to suffer the indignity of a woman telling them they were not good enough when the decisions were made for me. There were other decisions to be made. We were losing 5–1. The players had abandoned my instructed formation of 3–4–1–2 as soon as the second goal had gone in and reinvented themselves as a standard 4–4–2. They were like a piece of elastic that you can pull this way and that, but let it go and it reverts to how it was before you started meddling with it. English football is all about 4–4–2. You can see the brains of top professionals thumping against their temples when they play anything else.

'Are you playing 4–4–2 now?' I shouted at Lionel who was suddenly behaving like a left full back, having just headed in an own-goal of reasonably comic proportions. 'So much for my continental drift,' I yelled.

'Three at the back's out of fashion anyway,' he shouted back at me. I limped along the touch-line aware that as manager I ought to be exerting more control and coughing up tactical orders. But all I could think of in that first half was that the opposition were better than us. A peripheral member of our park side had automatically assumed the role of captain and was emitting all the usual clichés. 'Close 'im down, chase back, turn and face.'

'What does that *mean* exactly?' asked Kier, one of the park faithful who had babies to look after that day but had brought them along to watch us anyway. The self-appointed captain did set up our second goal with a beautifully timed pass, but for all his fighting talk was really rather frail in the tackle. By half-time our team was demoralised and all I could think of to say was that they had to call for the ball and support each other and try to play football instead of punting the ball wildly up the field. Did they listen to that? Maybe. The second half was much more enjoyable, and the social workers scored just the once because of a goalkeeping error. Our goalkeeper was poor. Lionel said he knew a goalkeeper who was keen to play but he may as well have said he knew a supermodel who was itching to be our cheerleader. It was not true. Mark looked most un-keen to be there and when I enquired as to what kind of goalkeeper he was, I was told that he had not played for seven years. Given that he looked about 17, the whole notion that he could justifiably be called a goalkeeper was laughable. But I should have known. Goalkeeper is often a euphemism for 'spindly and unfit' or 'fat and unpopular' or 'someone who will play anywhere and does not mind wearing a green and pink jersey'. If someone offers you a centre-half the chances are he has played a reasonable amount of soccer and knows what a defender should and should not do, but if someone offers you a keeper there is no way of knowing what you will get.

I was more voluble in the second half. I shouted out praise and barked that when we next took a corner, we should take a 'short one'. This order was obeyed and we looked more dangerous as a consequence. I had earlier yelled at Dave not to push up so far, and had been ignored, so the short corner response was immensely gratifying. I pictured myself at a post-match press conference being asked by top football correspondents what had pleased me most about the team's performance. 'They took a short corner after I had asked them to,' I would proudly reply and they would all laugh at my dry wit.

Before we kicked off I had gazed at the other matches being played along the stretch of Regent's Park between the zoo and the mosque that was a designated sports area. There was one rugby match in which the participants were all taller and more patrician-looking than the rest and the rest was all football. There were games defined by the racial mix and games defined by the lack of it. There were games with pace and games without it. There were games where from a distance you could see the players all swarm after the ball so it appeared as if they were playing tag in the playground rather than a sophisticated game requiring tactical acumen. Our match had elements of everything. It was dross peppered with little dabs of magic and pieces of individual endeavour which made me feel proud in a maternal sort of way.

The final score was 6–2 and an exultant social worker, the one with plaits, asked me to take a photograph of their team as it was only the second time they had won in 16 matches. I promised them a re-match when I was fit. They looked scared. Quite possibly they looked puzzled and I misread the signs, but there is only one way to exit after a comprehensive defeat and that is to be confident of winning next time. After all, they were social workers. When I told Graham, a long-lapsed member of our park gatherings, that we had been beaten by a bunch of social workers he could not guffaw long or loud enough. 'Yes,' I said resignedly, 'one of them did have his hair in plaits.' Later I turned to my husband, the rock at the heart of our defence, and told him we would play them again, maybe in three months time when my foot was better.

'You don't want to rush things,' he said. I ignored that.

'You never know,' I said, 'the next time we play them I might have one of my good matches. I might make a difference.'

'You want to make sure you're fully fit first though.'

'Yes, of course, but I could play well, it is possible, I mean, I might play better than Lionel, he didn't have one of his best games.'

Hubby smiled weakly. 'Yes dear.'

Frank needed seven stitches on the side of his head. 'The funny thing is,' he said a few days later. 'I've got a headache but the real problem is my leg. I picked up a grass burn and it's infected so I'm on antibiotics, but thanks for organising the game Ally.' It seems I misjudged the tactics, the opposition, and most of all my team's devotion to the cause. I should have been sacked, not profusely thanked for arranging it all.

CHAPTER TEN

initiation with Dog, Gary, Fatty and Slag

I read about it in a magazine. Women's football clubs were becoming increasingly popular. I felt ecstatic and stupid at the same time. There was I, simpering after the guys, weighed down by ball, pump and spare socks when all the time I could have been playing among equals. These clubs had youth teams and accepted girls as early as 11. By the time they were 20, I thought, they would be the finished article and I was envious. Today girls can play with boys at school or in after-school clubs and then, when they finish junior education, have the opportunity to join women-only teams. Actually I was simmeringly jealous. I became locked in a what-if scenario. If I had played football since I was three, I would by now be representing my country. If I had not had to start learning the game as a 23-year-old, I could have been sat at my desk with the blokes begging me to let them join my team. I would have looked glamorous in my replica Italy strip instead of gently pathetic.

I fantasised what life with a women's team would be like. I would be welcomed with open arms, another sister who understood the beautiful game. There would be a first team bulging with Amazons with benign gazes and a tough but fair coach. Life in the reserves would be fun and, if chosen to join the firsts, impish grins would send you on your way. Nevertheless I was nervous. It was like joining the brownies on your own halfway through term.

I opted, not unreasonably, to track down a team based near to where I lived. I found one which used Tottenham Hotspur's training facilities. I was not terribly fond of Spurs. I had formed an irrational dislike of them at around the age of five, and would even be torn as to what to hope for from a meeting between Tottenham and Manchester United, yet here I was driving up to the gates at White Hart Lane thinking, 'I'm a professional, I'm a professional,' with a big smirk on my face as I hauled my sports bag from the back seat. No autographs just now please. Ah, how the cocky crumble. I had stumbled on the club anyone who has ever had a sensitive disposition allied to a moderate-sized ego should go to to be cured of their personality.

There was aggression seeping from every pore of the place. It was splattered all over the changing-room walls and all over the women's faces. The girls were lingering in a state of half undress, deliberately ensuring that the boyfriends of those who had just been dropped off would see them in all their glory of shin-pads but no knickers, or Umbro shorts but no sports bra. There was much posturing. A piece of clothing seemed to be permanently in mid-air. They screamed and ranted.

'Where the fuck is my fucking shirt?'

'Where the fuck are my fucking boots?'

I dare say there is no need to list the full dialogue, as only the items missing altered from one mock-angry voice to the next. I felt desperately middle-class and far too happy with the world ever to fit in here. Would I only be able to play women's football as long as I was livid to the point of never-ending expletives? Still, they had the decency not to tell me to bugger off.

'What are you called?' I could tell instinctively this was not an invitation to tell them my name. I had already heard one girl addressed as 'Dog' as if it was as ordinary as Sue or Kate. There was a 'Gary' and a 'Fatty' and a 'Slag'. I, unfortunately, had only ever been given the nickname 'Crystal Tips'. That was at school and it had been meant as a cruel comment on how wild my hair was after the character in the cartoon *Crystal Tips and Alistair*. At the time I had thought it was rather sweet, however, but I knew that to suggest such a label now would invite derision, and it would quickly be altered to Ruby Tits or, more likely, just plain Tits.

'Ally,' I replied apologetically.

'We've already got one.'

'Er, Al then?' I was informed that would do even though it was boring. I was very aware suddenly that I had a posh voice, that I pronounced most of the letters in a word and had never uttered 'innit?' I don't usually think I have a posh voice, and in normal circumstances am quite pleased with my soft Lancashire accent, but at that moment I felt like I had just popped out of Daddy's chauffeur-driven limo having spent a year away at a finishing school near Lake Geneva. It was not just the words and the accents, it was body language, facial expression, eye contact. Everything I did seemed, to me, to be effete. I felt inadequate just tying my laces. My self-image had instantly become such that I felt I was sat there in a floaty white chiffon dress with pink ribbons on my sleeves. It was dawning on me that the guys

I played with were more feminine than this. These girls all seemed to have so much more energy, power and muscle – even the slim and pretty ones. They were a new species of hyper-women and I didn't even attempt to blend in; I would not have known how. I never watch *EastEnders* and I have never strutted around a town square in a gang wearing a mini-skirt in spite of it being minus three degrees making rude gestures to blokes and old grannies.

The coach was sick and I was impressed that the team opted to go through the training routines without an authority figure present. They had a routine and were set on auto-pilot to conform to it. Most members of the squad were younger than me and probably in their late teens. I believed, naïvely, it was necessary to prove I was every bit as fit as they and in the subsequent 50-yard dash was put up against the team captain. I did not know at that point that she was the captain, although I doubt it would have made any difference. I like to win and win I did. There was a stunned silence. Everyone gazed at their heroine as if all her hair had, in that precise moment, fallen out.

'That,' she announced, 'did not count. I was desperate for a fucking piss.'

Everyone laughed in relief. Somebody, unbelievably, actually said: 'Yeah, that's right she told me she was dying for the bog.' I wanted to say in that case let's re-run after she's had her fucking piss. But, of course, I said no such thing and I had the distinct impression that if I said anything at all no one would have heard me. The already sweaty and claustrophobic atmosphere of the indoor pitch was becoming almost unbearable. For the entire hour and a half I was there not one word was addressed to me, beyond the enquiry as to my name. It was as near to being invisible as I am likely to ever get. Even when I had won the race, no one looked at me, no one scowled at me, no one nudged me, no one told me to wise up. It put being blanked at a party into perspective.

Finally the football nets were dragged out and we bibbed up for a game. The standard was not as high as I had anticipated it would be. The emphasis seemed to be on crunching tackles and ensuring you went home with slide burns on the back of your thighs. We were a goal up, and the goalscorer appeared to be highly popular in a forced sort of way so I assumed she was the official centre forward and enjoyed all the status-trappings associated with such a position. Certainly it did not go down well with her when I scored the second. Perhaps she pouted, maybe she glared but for whatever reason her team-mates felt it necessary to disallow the goal. 'That never crossed the line,' someone yelled and everyone nodded in agreement. It was all I could do to stop myself gawping. These were players on my side, on my team, in the same yellow bibs deciding that a new player could not possibly upstage their temperamental star. I shook my head, silently snarled and ignored it, hoping that they had genuinely thought the ball had not crossed the line. But then I scored again. This time the ball flew into the back of the net and bounced back off the wall the goal leant against. You can't say that didn't cross the line, I muttered mentally.

'That rebounded off the cross-bar, that's not a goal,' shrieked Vivien Leigh's minder. I smiled. I couldn't help it. They were all mad, locked in a tiny society reminiscent of *Lord of the Flies*. They had created a new community with its own bizarre rules. There was a clear hierarchy, even hero-worship, but no deliberate cruelty. There was room for all shapes and sizes and for all levels of athletic ability – as long as no one expected any form of meritocracy. But I knew, had I opted for the 'Tits' nickname, spat on the changing room floor and then mooned out of the window, that my goals would have been greeted more appreciatively.

Soon the boyfriends returned having spent the evening locked in lesbian fantasy conversation in the pub. They were impervious to the language so presumably felt it to be entirely appropriate to the occasion. I left while the team dawdled in the showers and pretended to have good reason to stomp naked near the door. The fault is probably entirely mine and I am a prude. But I had been so entranced by the idea of an all-women team that I was annoyed at their mockery of it. It was as if they were asking to be belittled. In fact on reflection they were simply far too caught up in the comparison with men. They were in men's territory, playing a man's game and they thought that gave them the freedom to act as they assumed men did.

I have since been part of, or visited, other women's teams and none could quite live up to what I saw that evening. I have seen girls whose talent has not so much gone to their heads as taken over their body, mind and spirit. Their vanity knew no bounds. They argued constantly, found training an insult and, incredibly, were always on the verge of packing the game in. One would be shadowed everywhere by a trendily dressed fiancé who followed matches and training with a scary intensity and I am sure whispered in her ear down at the local pizzeria how much the team relied on her. I have met women who by contrast eat, sleep and drink football and would wither away and die if it was denied them. They were tough and masculine, short and stocky, but friendly enough. Some of the women I met deserved much more than they were ever likely to get. They played in the face of disapproval. One or two were on the verge of divorce. Some dashed home after training to put the kids to bed as their spouses were not about to help out of principle. There were the gigglers, almost more irritating than the whiners, who had no idea how they ended up playing in a women's team and would never in a million years understand what offside is. Playing against a team of gigglers is probably the most annoying experience of all time. One of them might try to cross and miss the ball altogether. Her response would be to put her hands to her face and laugh nervously. One might shoot and score. Her response would be to squeal and wave her arms about and look for her best mate, and most of them were studying sociology. There were the uncommunicatives, the rabbiters, and the goaders, but the White Hart Lane girls topped the lot. They were, for once, in control and if you didn't want to see your girlfriend's best pal's bottom then sod off. Needless to say the boyfriends stayed and I did not return.

I rushed back into the arms of my boys. Compared to the disillusionment of that initiation, the men's early taunts of a woman ruining their game had been positively seductive. 'It was horrible,' I told them, but the lads heard the words, White, Hart and Lane and then stopped listening. They were all jealous or indignant that I had trained at Spurs. What struck me, as I nestled in the bosom, or rather beer-belly, of my footballing family, was how effortlessly the men played. The girls had given it all so much energy;

even when attempting to look indifferent they had been concentrating hard. For a few weeks I sank into sexism and tried to forget I was female and ought to be seeking out another women's team. I am perfectly happy with the men in the park I told myself, and I was happy, but the existence of women's teams had come between us, the way the existence of a forest comes between a boy and a captive fox. My team-mates cast me glances that said, 'Run, run, little one, run free with the girls and excel, don't accept the safe captivity we have made for you. Fend for yourself.' And, after a couple of matches in which I finished the joint worst player, I remembered fondly that, in spite of everything, while with the women I was faster and sharper.

I had my boss to thank for a second chance. He was a local councillor and had been instrumental in allowing a Football in the Community style grant to be applied to a women's team. That team was Leyton Orient Ladies; their base was a 15-minute walk from my home. I was interested but understandably terrified. A few days after mentioning this team, my boss told me he had contacted the club to warn them of my imminent arrival. He assured me that they had assured him they were extremely positive toward newcomers, especially ones who were over 18 and had played before.

Part of me was relieved my path had been smoothed, but I was also irritated at being made to feel like a child. It was like being eight again and having your mum phone the school to complain about her daughter's treatment in the choir. 'She may very well have been off-key throughout "All Things Bright and Beautiful", headmaster, but more fool you for giving the children such an appalling song.'

Unsurprisingly I turned up at Leyton Orient Ladies with the wide-eyed nervousness of just such an eight-year-old. I arrived in full kit this time, no more gratuitous bare bottoms for me, and came face to face with a scene from some sci-fi future world. A couple of dozen strapping young men were lapping a large fenced and floodlit arena. The inside of the arena was Astroturfed and it had four sets of five-a-side goals. Outside there was mud and only the deflected light of the arena's lamps. Inside several separate groups of women and girls were hard at work engaged in dribbling around cones or taking turns to shoot at goal; outside the men groaned as if on a chain gang and they tried keepy-uppy with their boots flicking mud into their faces which were distorted by the half-light. Men are low-life, women are our athletic future, seemed to be the plot of this sci-fi film, and I cheered up enormously as I approached someone who looked as though they might be in charge.

I feared either scenario, the one where they pretended I did not exist, never counted the goal I had just scored, and the one where they ushered me to the front of the queue, whispering that their grant might be in jeopardy if I was not picked for the first team.

The truth was, happily, somewhere in between. It certainly helped that the chap who ran the club had been told about me, but only in so far as I was offered a degree of welcome and more people seemed to know my name than would have been the case anywhere else. The name Ally was not sneered at, quite the reverse in fact, for none of the girls there had nicknames and once, when comfortably accepted into the fold, I even had a little tantrum and said I would not pass to anyone who forgot my name was Ally and not Alyson.

They take paperwork very seriously at Leyton Orient Ladies. Before I could even stretch my hamstring, let alone kick a ball, I was warned about the importance of FA registration, players' injury insurance, and there was a lengthy debate about my eligibility to play for LOL at all. I was told I would have to apply for an official transfer from the team of Dog, Fatty and Slag before I could begin training as there were fines imposed for the poaching of players from other women's teams. It took a while, but in the end they accepted I had never actually belonged to Dog, Fatty and Slag, I had just suffered there and they pointed to the group I would train with.

LOL is one of the better-organised and longer-standing women's clubs. They had a first team, a reserve team and a transition team, which was full of bursting acne and teenage angst since it catered for girls too old to remain in the youth teams, but too stroppy to represent the elite firsts. LOL also had a melting-pot side. This was where I was plonked. It ostensibly existed for outsiders. LOL was cruising with an assembly line which groomed girls in the youth teams to eventually play for the firsts. Anyone new to the system or unknown to the club were shown to the Casuals. As its name implied it was also home to players who had been through the system but disliked the regimentation. If you could only play one weekend in four, the chances were, you could get a game with the Casuals.

I joined halfway through the season and it was all a bit of a mess. We played anyone in London who needed a game; our manager was often too busy to turn up, and although there was a core attendance at training, someone different turned up every week and then promptly disappeared. At the end of my first training session, someone wandered over with a piece of paper which stated we had a pitch booked for a home match, so we had better make sure we made use of it. There was much debate as to whom we would play but an opposition was found remarkably promptly, and then Mark, our coach, asked Karen, our captain, to sort out who was available. It was, with hindsight, pretty naff stuff, we were not even in a league, but I was terribly excited.

'Would you be able to play, Ally?' asked Karen.

I tried to sound blasé. 'If you need me, yes, sure.'

So the following Sunday I arrived back at the club. There were only 11 of us, so I was in the team. This upset the hierarchy and Beth the boss popped her head round the dressing-room door to inform me that it was most unusual, not to say undesirable, for such a newcomer to be given a game so quickly. 'Don't think you'll be playing every week,' she said sternly. Ally the eight-year-old just nodded, overwhelmed by the occasion.

Our coach was playing in his own match and so Karen and her boyfriend Kev, were put in charge for the afternoon.

'You can play as centre forward,' Karen told me 'because you are tall.' I am five foot six and a bit, but it was true, compared to my new team-mates I was a veritable goddess. My stomach churned with nerves as, awe-struck, I pulled on a Leyton Orient jersey. It took only twenty minutes for the stars to be swiped from my star-struck demeanour. The opposition were awful and as Karen and I jogged towards the ball, which had become lodged three inches from the goal-line inside the six-yard box Karen, who reached the ball first said, 'You have this one Ally, I've already got two goals.'

'No, no really, after you, it's your hat-trick after all,' I responded.

God knows where the goalkeeper was during this existential argument in front of her goal. I felt crumpled by the sheer amateurishness of it all and had time to reflect upon the irony of being offered a goal when the main reason for joining a women's team was to play among equals, for a chance to excel and not feel that the man marking me might have tried harder had I not been a woman. When I took off my shirt it was not even dusty from its languid exertions and I felt generally deflated. This was one football dream which had been blown horribly off course.

CHAPTER ELEVEN

Elaine the Enigma and the Dwarf Keeper

'So, how was the big match?' asked Sean.

'I played as a striker,' I said proudly, conveniently forgetting my disillusionment. I should not have admitted my role for the next question was obvious.

'And did you score?'

'Yes, I mean, no.' I shrugged. 'It was a weird game.'

Karen had even offered the option that we should simultaneously kick the ball over the line. It was extremely nice of her, I know, and in many respects she represented the antithesis of what befell me at White Hart Lane and I should have been grateful. But really. I could not have told any of the guys about it. It would have resulted in jibes as to whether we dashed off at half-time to find some heated tongs to restore the curls in our hair, and whether we powdered our noses before taking a corner. And anyway have two players ever been jointly awarded a goal, neither claiming it for themselves and all the evidence pointing to a joint kick of equal power? I shuddered at the thought of it.

Such an inglorious start had a clear consequence. The girls had not stolen my heart. It was February and so the men and I were still playing under floodlights in Bayswater on Thursday evenings. Thursday was also the night the ladies of the Orient trained. Training began at 7.30 p.m. in Walthamstow, east London. My six-a-side match finished at 7 p.m. If I dashed straight to the tube after the game and was lucky with connections, I calculated, I would miss only half an hour of a 90-minute session. This was in an era when it was still cold in February. I would start thawing out on the train and then sprint up and down escalators and then hit a blast of cold air again as I emerged in east London. The jog from the station to the club, with my sports bag hanging off my shoulder, was the most tortuous part of the whole journey. The first time I arrived late and breathless I thought would be my last. There was no way a new player would be allowed to miss the first half an hour of training, certainly not when that first half hour comprised the nasty bits; the running and the exercises. But I was fortunate that our coach, Mark, was impressed that I was late because I had been playing football.

'Come on you lazy lot,' he would shout at my team. 'Why can't you be super-fit like Ally here?' Favouritism? I did not think so as I agreed with Mark that my antics were highly commendable but one or two of my team-mates pouted. Mark would set up complex routines aimed at improving our skills and then divide us into teams for a quick match towards the end of the session. His word was final. He accepted a bit of cheek but knew where to draw the line. He was 17.

When we learned it was soon to be his 18th birthday, there was much excitement. Turning 18 in east London is, apparently, a big deal. We had a series of top-secret meetings to organise a surprise for him. None of the suggestions was very pleasant, but the plan which caused us most mirth was for a woman, wearing a football kit, to approach him in the bar after training, and ask him if she could join our team. She would then proceed to take her kit off revealing the standard garb; stockings, suspenders and so on and perform the standard demeaning acts. It was a horrible plan but the theory and the way we planned it, was fun. Not one of us suggested that a group of women should not really be paying another woman to degrade herself, and maybe I was the only one who thought about this.

As soon as the strippagram arrived my heart sank. She was too old and too tarty, so the deception part of the ruse, the only amusing part, was unlikely to work. She wore a lilac shell suit and deep red lipstick and carried a can of ready whipped cream. Mark was horrified and turned crimson. The girls shrieked as his nose was pushed into a cleavage full of St Ivel. He was never the same after that. He took less lip at training and soon after left us for good. We were panic-stricken. Mark had been a poor and frequently absent manager, but a good coach. However, his leaving prompted a reorganisation. If we, the Casuals, were to survive, we had to enter the women's league and attract a committed manager. The candidate was obvious. Every week Karen's fiancé turned up to watch her train, discuss tactics in the bar and watch us play on Sundays. Kev was approached and suitably honoured to be asked. Kev and Karen were amazing. She was 17, he was 33. Her parents approved and so did we. Kev was sensible, caring and successful, and generous. Karen represented everything I thought I despised in womanhood – her ambition was to have a big wedding, become a housewife and then a mother. Two months before her wedding she gave up football and never returned. Yet she was energetic, charismatic, athletic and honest. She was so sure about Kev that she did not mind how much time he spent with us, her female team-mates. I was, in truth, a little in awe of her. She was even mature and honest enough to tell me that at first she had thought I was flirtatious, and that troubled her slightly, but now she knew me better she realised that I was just talkative and liked my footie.

Towards the end of my first half-season with the Orient votes were cast for our team's player of the year. I was eligible to vote even though I had not witnessed, let alone played in, most of the matches, but did not know it. Karen told me about the procedure. She was in the running for player of the season, indeed I expected her to run away with it and I told her so. She frowned and said that Jenny, our left full-back, had attracted lots of votes and it was very close. 'So, if you want me to win the award,' she said, 'you had better get your vote in. Give it to me and I'll lodge it for you if you can't make the meeting tonight.' I could never have pulled that off. Karen managed to make it clear she wanted the award and needed my vote and yet she did not appear desperate, vain or egotistical, just honest.

The Orient's season ended and I carried on playing football in the park. They had briefly overlapped, the park and the Orient, and the plan was always that I would play for an hour with the boys and then do my *Mission Impossible* routine to make training with the girls. But too often the game in the park was too sumptuous to leave, and knowing that the boys would play for maybe another hour after I had left was too much to bear. I felt guilty but guilty in a 'I've eaten all the champagne truffles and left only the congealed coffee creams' sort of way. Playing was far preferable to training.

The new season with the Orient was splendid. We had an organised fixture list and a new set of shirts. I moved into central midfield because Kev decided my strength was my passing ability and I would be able to set up goals. But, having played all my previous football with men, the central midfield had been forbidden territory. It was the place for power and presence. Now I was being offered control of it. I responded with a puff of pride that turned me in my mind's eye into a colossus. I felt two feet taller and two feet broader than any other woman on the pitch. I decided I had to win every ball and so I did. I sprang high to head the ball clear, I slid in to dispossess then jumped up to run with the ball before passing into the path of the striker. I ignored how exhausted I felt and worked harder than I've ever worked to make the midfield my territory.

Ladies football is still in its infancy and as a consequence teams compete against each other when they have no right to do so. We have been overwhelmed, outclassed and embarrassed one week and dominant to the point of a 19–0 scoreline the next. But this, my first match as a midfield maestro, was a close game. We were in almost every respect on a par and that was what made it so memorable. My determination made the difference. It also opened my team-mates' eyes to the possibility that I was more than just a blonde prima donna who liked impersonating Matthew Le Tissier. Guts. That is the quality women footballers admire and to their astonishment, I had it. Kev was pleased, too. He had seen my potential in a midfield role and had been proven correct.

At the time I had not done much of the day-dreaming

that accompanies so much of my football. Often, just as a corner is being taken, I will imagine the stunning goal I want to be able to score. But for this match I had been too absorbed and too exhausted to think about anything other than 'the ball is mine'. I did not therefore feel particularly pleased with myself when the full-time whistle was blown. I had done my job and hoped I had done it well. The referee shook my hand and in a low voice said, 'You were impressive.' Then, after we had changed, Kev said something along the lines of me being the jewel in the crown of a fine team performance – you don't have to be on telly to utter football clichés. Karen joined him, 'Ally, everyone's decided you were man of the match.'

Word spread around the club. At training the following Thursday Beth the boss said: 'I hear you played well.' I was pleased, of course, but glory for me until then had been so wrapped up with one-off moments, a goal or the pass that led to a goal that I was genuinely surprised by all the attention. What shook me from this alien demeanour of modesty was the match report.

The real Leyton Orient give the ladies space in the club's match-day programme. On Saturday 31 October 1992, in the programme devoted to Orient's home game against Swansea it said, 'Midfielder Alyson Rudd was outstanding for the Casuals in their 1–0 win over University College London.' It was so rare for anyone other than goalscorers to be mentioned, let alone feted. Shelley, an Orient fan, gave me a copy of the programme and I pinned it next to my Liverpool calendar on the wall in the office. Whenever I felt low I glanced up at it. Just the description 'midfielder' was enough to send little quivers of pride down my aorta.

It was a crucial episode. I was touched by the generosity

of praise and I moved out of the ranks of newcomer into the department of players whose name goes down first on the team-sheet. It also resulted in LOL becoming a higher priority in my own football hierarchy. Meanwhile girls came and went. Most were in pairs. They arrived in pairs, left in pairs and while with us they gossiped in pairs. Occasionally a pair would fall out, more likely than not because one was picked for the team and the other was squeezed in as a sub. One such pair were Tracy and Carol. Quite how they were ever a pair in the first place, I never found out. Tracy was in her mid-twenties and arrived for training and games in a four-year-old Jag, driven by her husband, John, whom she talked about and treated as if he was a boyfriend of two weeks' standing. For John's sake she arrived plastered in make-up. Now I have worn mascara while playing football and so have many other women, but Tracy wore the full encyclopaedia. She wore tinted foundation cream and powder, blusher, lipstick and eye-shadow. On the rare occasions she did play I cringed as the opposition stared at her then whispered they must be about to face real buttercups. Tracy could have been the most skilful player in the city, she wasn't, but would never have looked it. The streaked blonde hair, tied back carefully with a velvet ribbon, the suspiciously ironed football shirt, the Candy Pearl lip gloss all undermined the vigour of a sporting pursuit.

Her friend Carol wore no make-up and her hair always seemed in need of a wash. She was in the closing stages of acne and had a moustache. Carol was energetic. All her footballing knowledge deserted her as soon as we kicked off and she simply scampered around the pitch giving away free kicks, refusing to accept there is such a thing as offside, until she either scored or was pulled off for being too great a nuisance. Only when they both left did I realise I may have misjudged them. Tracy was risking divorce from her 'a woman's place is in the bedroom' husband for trying a hobby in the first place and Carol was an ambitious artist. Someone had challenged Tracy about the make-up and had been told that John really did not like to see his woman leave the house without making an effort with her appearance. It sounded sinister and I regretted not making more of an effort to understand her. Carol knew all about it and that presumably was what knitted their friendship together.

We rarely had a settled side but the closest we came was in that first season under Kev's guidance. In men's amateur football the position of goalkeeper is a perennial problem as anyone who is any good wants to be out there contributing as part of the team, but at LOL there were lots of women who would never be any good but had to be accommodated somehow. Teaching them how to keep goal was the solution. That we always seemed to have a different goalkeeper was due more to there being a surfeit of them needing match practice than a crisis of availability.

Our left full-back was always Jenny. She was short, short even for a short woman but extremely good at being a left-back. In fact she could not and would not play anywhere else. Once Kev asked her to play on the left side of midfield and it was the only time the normally shy, gentle, good-natured Jenny ever lost her temper. It is, though, a left-back trait as opposed to a feminine one. Gary, the left-back from the park, is such a superb player that when I have organised 11-a-side games I have attempted to put him in central defence or in midfield. Gary has never lost his temper on these occasions, but as the game unfolds he gravitates towards the left touchline.

Elaine was always our right-sided midfielder. Elaine was something of an enigma. She had played with men too, but rarely spoke of it. She smoked a cigarette just before kick-off, at half-time and at the final whistle. Beth the boss saw her one afternoon and issued a declaration that anyone again found smoking while wearing an Orient shirt would be heavily fined for bringing the game and the team into disrepute. Elaine started smoking behind the changing-room walls but after the fuss had died down could be found soliciting for fags among the opposition at half-time. We were hardly amazed that Elaine complained about exhaustion and wheezed throughout the team-talks, but she somehow managed to maintain an impressive level of acceleration throughout the 90 minutes. She was also skilful. We relied on her for all our set pieces and I envied her confident nonchalance as she placed the ball in front of a wall of six women. She was our best penalty taker and on her day could beat three challenges and put in a pinpoint cross. My happiest hours were spent playing in midfield and dashing forward when Elaine had the ball, knowing she would beat her marker and float the ball to my feet. I would score and dance over to her to thump her on the back while she hacked up some phlegm and complained of the stitch in her side. For three seasons running Elaine and I were neck and neck in the race to see who would finish top goalscorer.

Elaine was the only member of my team I ever really wanted to know better. I admired her skill and unselfishness. She made me laugh and she was intelligent, taking time out from being a social worker to take another degree. But her overall air of indifference applied to me too, and having spent an evening in my Bayswater flat suffering my hyper hospitality she drifted away from me during circuit training and friendship never blossomed.

Another social worker, Sally, spent a season with us. She was incredibly self-deprecatory and occasionally, if she was feeling brave, she would question her inclusion in the team. I once gave her a lift home and gleaned from her that she would not be back the following September.

'Are you joining another team?' I asked. She laughed and said she was giving it up because she was not good enough and because she did not like competitive sport. 'Oh,' I said, understandably confused. 'So why are you here at all?' Sally's answer was that was she was taking a political stance. She approved of women making inroads into a male sport and wanted to support her sisters in the struggle. 'I feel it is my duty,' she told me 'but I really don't have a good time. I quite like the training but I hate the games and all that pressure on you to kick the ball before the other girl gets there first.' Sally was a feminist, socialist, non-confrontationalist and being torn up inside. For the rest of the season I made an extra effort to shout well done whenever she cleared the ball out of defence. For Sally must have felt like a vegetarian eating veal and when she was booked for a late tackle she must have felt as guilty as if she had just binged at McDonalds.

The Casuals also usually had to find a position for 'Sarge'. 'Sarge' was what we used instead of an Afro-Caribbean name that I never saw written down but I think was Sanja. Sarge was not only the sole black member of our side but deaf to boot. Everyone said they were not being racist, indeed they argued that they were being too non-racist and that if Sarge had been white they might not have tolerated her presence. The problem was that the local borough had a team for deaf women. This was incredibly far-sighted of them. Very few councils trouble to consider women's football but to consider women who are deaf might want to play too ... But Sarge did not want to be treated as a disabled minority. The standard of the deaf women was poor, she complained and LOL was closer to her home.

It represented a dilemma. Sarge was extremely personable. She went out of her way to make up for her lack of communication skills by identifying which team you supported and then grunting the appropriate score of their last match when she saw you at training. Everyone shouted at her but I was not at all sure that helped, as she only seemed to understand you if she was halfway to guessing the point. Sarge had flair but was frustrating to play with as she never heard you call for the ball, never heard a warning of an impending tackle and never looked up to see who she might pass to. This last failing was not a direct consequence of her disability but more to do with a lack of confidence. If only she could learn to look up, all her other problems would disappear but she rarely did. Just once she played a blinder and I am sure I saw a tear form in the corner of her eye as we streaked forward to congratulate her on a splendid, swerving shot that gave us the lead. More often than not she was sub and we all moaned when she came on.

Yvonne was by turns a keeper and a defender. She was a quite splendid sweeper, with a commanding air and awareness of our defensive frailties, but Yvonne was desperate to play in goal. Often she would leave us and play for the first team reserves if their keeper was unavailable.

Perhaps we should all have just let her play where she so wanted to but Yvonne was five foot tall. Quite why she ever wanted to pull on a pair of goalkeeper's gloves again having been lobbed five times inside 30 minutes, no one ever knew, but it was the only time I ever saw her smile.

Yvonne's children accompanied her everywhere. There was an unwritten rule that kids should not be allowed to interfere with training but also an unwritten rule that Yvonne's were the exception. They were lovely kids, cheeky but well-behaved and there was a fierce one-parent-family bond between them and their mum.

The misery-guts of the side was Amanda. She badly wanted to be captain and latterly she was, but in my opinion it was a mistake. In common with many women, what might have sounded like authoritative presence in a small room became a comical, hollow shriek on the wide open spaces of a football field. If we were losing she became apoplectic and frequently actually lost her voice by the end of a game. Her failing was that she picked on errors rather than effort and her position was continually undermined by her lack of ability. Amanda did not like me one bit. She arrived almost a year and a half after I did and I was reasonably warm and friendly toward her as I tried to be toward any newcomer. But she took exception to my pleasantries, and then to the way I played, and then to the fact I was always picked for the team. She quickly tried to create her own power base and her zenith came when her boyfriend took over as our manager and he dropped me to the subs bench for missing training the previous Thursday. I was appalled, particularly as I had given the team a month's notice that I could not get to training, but Alan, goaded by Amanda, was adamant I needed to be punished. Unfortunately for Amanda I came on after 25 minutes and promptly scored two goals. Alan and Amanda split up three weeks later and her moods became harrowing. If she ever laughed I missed it. Later still Amanda tried another insurrection, during pre-season five-a-sides which I usually missed, preferring Regent's Park, but she misjudged her popularity and our then new player/manager Rachel, her latest target, survived.

Rachel arrived six weeks after me and I mistook her for a member of the Under-16 squad even though she was the same age as me. As soon as she spoke the years piled upon her. Rachel had no girlishness in her. She had suffered a tough childhood and a debilitating adolescence, but had pulled herself around and was now married and in a managerial post. Rachel had the unnerving effect of making me feel 13. She was so sensible and serious and, unlike Amanda, was grateful for my early friendliness. We were opposites in every way, but after a couple of months and after she had given me a couple of lifts to the station, we became one of the pairs I used to laugh at.

Rachel thought I needed taking down a peg or two and usually succeeded in this by confiding in me how unpopular I was but she also let some element of admiration sneak into our friendship and so it survived. Perhaps she thought she was taking me under her wing for her other close friend was Lucy. Lucy was pretty with close auburn curls and an expressive face. The first time I played alongside her she regaled me with apologies for how terrible she had been and did I mind being in the same side as she was. I told her she had been great and was pulled to one side by Karen who told me Lucy was 'not well'. Gradually over the next five years stories about Lucy emerged, that Lucy had attempted suicide, that Lucy was suffering first this psychiatric disorder and then that. But apart from that first conversation Lucy seemed to me to be perfectly normal. In fact she was one of the more pleasant and intelligent women I played with. After a perfectly jolly two hours in the club bar or over a pizza, Lucy would leave and then Rachel would sigh about how worried she was for Lucy's safety and fill me in about midnight mercy dashes to her 'protected dwelling' or ask me if I noticed how anorexic she looked.

It was all very bizarre as if women's football attracted people in need of therapy for their marriage or their health or their self-esteem or their very existence. But then when I thought about the oddities in Regent's Park and the number of professional players in therapy I realised the girls were not so odd after all.

CHAPTER TWELVE

scoring from the halfway line

The Casuals were looked upon with varying degrees of humour or distaste by the rest of the club. We were the dumping ground for anyone who came from the outside or anyone whose job meant they could not be available for every match. Although all the different teams trained alongside each other I knew very few girls outside of my team.

As if sensing that an element of unhealthy rivalry was permeating the teams, Beth the boss cajoled us to join in the Tuesday night training. 'It's for everyone at the club, not just the first team,' she said and I was sure she was looking at me.

Tuesday was as serious as Thursday was a farce. There was a lot of hanging about on a Thursday, lots of queuing to take a turn at a shot, lots of debate about where the cones should be set up and who should be on whose side for the shuttle races. Tuesdays, Beth had promised, would improve our match performances by a mile.

Only a fifth of the women eligible to do so turned up on Tuesdays. It was the flip side of Thursdays with the men training inside the floodlit pitch and us on the perimeter.

We began with a pacy jog around the Astroturf fence, then we warmed up with stretching exercises and then we sprinted. There was always an element of competition, someone was always sick. Rod, the specialist Tuesday coach, thought he was losing his touch unless someone retched into the mud.

There was an other-worldliness to these sessions. We were all half-obscured in darkness and if our sprints were over ambitious and we ran too far from the fencing, we were completely enveloped by the night. Rod was all-powerful, even Beth succumbed to his authority. He barked out scathing criticism more often than praise and had the measure of us all. It was as if he could see into our souls. He understood very quickly who simply could not run fast and who could if threatened. He knew I only ran fast in a race and tried to encourage me to put more effort into the less competitive elements of training.

After an hour of physical torture, we practised ball skills. I was often the only Casual there and would become nervous of being shown up to be a poor excuse for a footballer but usually I fared reasonably well. I took it all so seriously that when Rod set us homework I feverishly attempted to comply and I remember the puzzled look on my parents' faces as I unsmilingly practised keepy-uppy in their garden. Yes, I could conjure up a Cruyff turn, but only when Rod blew his whistle, never in a real game.

Rod even realised that part of the reason for my regular attendance could be because I had developed a slight fancy for him. It was only slight and based purely on his unrelenting control of us women but having engaged in eye contact a fraction too long as we all 'warmed down' in the changing rooms, Rod gratuitously explained that his wife would be picking him up that evening. I stopped air cycling and let my legs drop with a thud to the floor. One second before I had been a pliable unquestioning pupil, now I was fed up stretching this and stretching that. Rod noticed the sudden if subtle change and roared: 'Keep up Ally, it's not all getting too much for you is it?'

I smiled. 'I think I'll cope,' I said and with that the mini-crush was crushed, but I still turned up on Tuesdays. It became addictive. If I missed a session my body screamed accusingly at me, and Beth the boss was right, match-days were a breeze. Here, I was at the peak of my commitment fitting in two matches and two training sessions a week. For some incalculable reason I decided the woman who operated the cappuccino machine in the sandwich bar near my office had to come to training too. I did not know her beyond thanking her for my change as she sneered at the next customer. In fact she was so dour she fascinated me. She was incredibly attractive in a Meryl Streep sort of way and the more I smiled the more she frowned. After months of snubbing my bubbly 'good mornings' she took me to one side.

'Why,' she hissed, 'are you so nice to me?' I realised I had no idea.

'I just thought you needed cheering up,' I said. A friendship grew out of a few exchanged words every week day. She was Polish and married to a possessive Italian. I learned she was athletic and began the pestering.

'Come to my football training, you'll love it.' Three months later her husband gave her permission to go with me.

The first shock was seeing her outside the sandwich bar. She was short. The eastern European goddess had vanished along with the raised platform she worked on inside the shop. The second was her intensity. 'No one has ever been nice to me in England, you are my only friend, I trust you.' The third was the way she left my team-mates open-mouthed at her incredible fitness and flexibility. She smiled sardonically as she completed the splits and I beamed hoping to bask a little in her reflected glory. 'She's my friend.'

Beth the boss was unimpressed and scolded me for just turning up with someone without telling her about it but when I explained she was house-bound and this was likely to be her only visit, Beth softened. Beth knew there were lots of women who risked an almighty row every time they turned up for training.

I went to Magda's house for supper and soon realised I was meddling in things I did not understand. Magda was so strong-willed, so sullen on the one hand and so willing to please her miniature husband on the other. Buoyed by my faith in her she left the cappuccinos and worked for a wholesaler and then for a magazine and fretted about fulfilling her potential. I felt responsible for making her question her life and her husband eyed me with contempt. For the remaining Tuesdays I was quiet as before. The hard-core of the women were local, real East Enders who all knew each other from school or the job centre. I casually slipped in the odd 'innit' but I was an outsider in every sense with my accent, my education, my job, even my build.

The club's policy of developing youngsters was starting to pay off and some talented girls were emerging into the first team from the youth squad. This naturally had repercussions. Women who had been in the first team for years and knew everyone and everything about the club were suddenly being usurped. There were constant flare-ups about who was picked and who was not. The club tried to resolve the problem by creating a team just for starlets but it was fraught with temper tantrums itself and various managers found the task daunting and for a while no one wanted anything to do with them.

For a while some joined us. They thought it was beneath them; we thought they should go elsewhere, and after a match in which they behaved abominably they were told to pack it all in or change their attitude. I caught a starlet complaining to a member of the opposition that she just could not cope playing alongside such incompetents. She then proceeded to pass only to her fellow starlets and to groan far too audibly whenever a regular Casual made a mistake. This was our team, we were making room for Orient's brightest future stars and this was the thanks we got. I was enraged by their ignorance and ego. Their manager was on hand and heard it all but issued only the mildest rebuke which was in itself an insult. 'Please, Kelly, I know it's difficult but try to enjoy it.'

Of all the people I have played with I truly detested only these. They were skilful, young and promising but also lazy, self-centred and without grace. It undermines everything that is good about team sport when it turns your stomach to see one of your own team score a goal. Sometimes we were joined by Orient girls moving in the opposite direction either because their work meant they could not exhibit first team commitment or because age had slowed them down. They fared better and if they felt scornful they knew better at least than to show it.

The biggest prima donna of all the starlets was Carrie. She was half-Italian, tall and long-limbed. Everyone drooled over her, for in a game where all was seemingly lost, Carrie would bewitch a full-back, cut in and effortlessly score. I dread to think what happened to Carrie in the real world. She was fairly beautiful, fairly stupid and stupendously petulant. She emitted the strangest low-pitched whine and for several months I thought she did not speak any English. But she did, of course, if only to complain that she felt ill or had pulled a muscle or was no good. This she did in order to be told by any number of doting club officials and team-mates that she was fantastic. But maybe I am being uncharitable. I played against her twice in a couple of games arranged during the summer. No doubt the occasions were too pedestrian for her but I saw not one glimmer of her star quality. Presumably she was suffering a calf strain. It was when I met girls like Carrie that I understood how women's football could become a ghastly mistake. If it were to take off, to attract money and supporters and extensive television coverage then there would be hundreds of Carries, all tanned, all with extra long eyelashes and all missing the point of a team sport.

The Casuals finished just below mid-table under Kev's stewardship. Sometimes we had the use of the club's new mini-bus to ferry us to away fixtures. These journeys were intimidating. At the last minute the more likeable members of my team would contact us to say they would make their own way to the ground and I would be left sat among the pairs, and younger pairs at that, who would giggle at bottom jokes and chew gum. Sometimes the journey would take two hours and if we were travelling in convoy one car would always get lost. Often the away pitch would be in the middle of an awesome sports complex with several men's football games and a couple of rugby matches all being played at the same time, and we would be steered into a changing room that the men had just vacated and be half overcome with the stench of sweat clinging to the benches and clothes pegs.

The kit bag was thrown into the middle of the changing room and someone, usually whoever had washed them, would pluck the shirts out and toss them into the air. This caused me great anxiety. I had to have the number 10 shirt. I was fortunate that many of the girls knew relatively little about football and did not understand what the number 10 shirt signified; namely that I am a vain, self-important player who thinks the team relies on my play-making skill and judgement. At the time that was not what I thought. I just wanted it in the same way as a child wants a Smartie *now* and will not be deflected by promises of a biscuit later. But it was a vain desire, it must have been, for although it became superstitious it started out as my ability firstly to manipulate the women into letting me have the shirt, and then to have the shirt that says to anyone watching, hey she must be good, she's their number 10.

Once, when Lisa drifted down from the reserves to play for us, she grabbed the number 10. She had not been the number 10, I was sure of that, no, she thought as she had played at a nominally higher level she ought to be represented by the classy digits. I made a strangulated 'uuhh' noise and held my arms out, waiting for Karen or Jenny to help me out. 'Does it matter?' said Karen. I grimaced and told them it mattered if they wanted me to play well. Yvonne laughed: 'What makes you think you play well when you do wear it?' Of course I had to pretend that was funny. 'Ha, ha. I'll play worse then, so bad that you'll be begging me always to have it.' Lisa was by now pulling the shirt on over her head and I was very close to tears as the number 5 was missing and the only shirt left was number 12. In the end Rachel intervened and said, 'Oh go on, let her wear it, we need her to play well so make sure you do Ally.'

When Amanda joined the team she was unsurprisingly horrified that I was allowed to grab the number 10 shirt and started babbling on about the team wearing it on a rotation basis – she was terribly right-on as well as miserable. But, because no one really wanted it as badly as I did, I usually wore it. And I loved that feeling, of walking in the vaguely butch way studs on boots make a girl walk, out of the changing rooms and toward the pitch, the number 10 on my back telling the world I must be all right. Had they stuck around to watch they could have been disappointed for I was almost as inconsistent with the women as I am with the men. I was never substituted, however. Whoever was in charge lived in hope, as I did, that I would come good in the end.

Occasionally not even the coveted 10 could make up for what awaited us on our travels. One team we played, albeit in a friendly rather than a league game, was so awful I scored from the halfway line, chipping the keeper, yards off her line, and as we were 7–0 up there seemed no reason not to attempt what would normally be considered an audacious shot. The other side were scared to tackle, scared of the ball, scared of our red shirts, scared, quite probably, of moving onto solids. There was no satisfaction to be derived from this kind of game. We were not tired at the end and all the great individual skill was nothing when put into perspective.

One team, in our league, simply failed to show up on

their home turf. We waited and waited and eventually their captain cycled toward us and said none of them had wanted to get out of bed. They were subsequently kicked out of the league, but all we had to show for our efforts was a hastily assembled match between ourselves and a couple more late risers on a pitch that sloped so steeply it is by now no doubt a dry ski run.

Just as Liverpool have Manchester United and Leeds have Manchester United, we had a team we loved to hate. They were West Ham Ladies. I was told to hate them of course, I had no prior reason to, and the reason for the hatred was bound up with West Ham poaching some of the Orient girls in order to establish themselves. The Orient girls were not hit over the head, bound and gagged and dragged to West Ham but, no matter, we hated them. Also, they kept beating us. And, as is the way in football, we kept meeting them in cup competitions and all sorts of friendly fixtures, for although we hated them we pretended to be all East End girls together.

Such was the rivalry that for one game against the Hammers Karen and Kev and a few other girls had rounded up a posse of supporters. There were white haired grannies, trendy mates from college and a couple of gormless 13-year-old boys lined up along the touchline with their butties and lemonade to cheer us on. The night before I had been on a first date with an economist called Adrian, and we had spent a good hour and a half of that date discussing goalscoring technique. Adrian had described the shot that keepers find most irksome, the one where the striker places the ball to the side of the keeper so that it runs under where their waist will be as they fall and stretch to save it. 'I'll try that tomorrow,' I told him, sure that I wouldn't because most of the women keepers I faced were not sophisticated enough to realise they were being outwitted.

But West Ham had a new keeper. She was odd looking. She was tall. She was athletic and she was extremely good. We flooded forward in a burst of indignant derby match energy and tried shots that in any other game would have put us 3–0 up but this girl effortlessly claimed them all. They then went 3–0 ahead and our bottom lips began to tremble, as you will have seen many a famous player's lip tremble in similar circumstances. Then I received the ball from Elaine just inside their half. I was immediately challenged but I pushed the ball past my opponent and sprinted forward. I could hear the grannies squeal in delight and, unaccustomed to having the crowd, any crowd, behind me, I pelted up the pitch. A couple more challenges failed and I was one on one with supergirl-keeper. I remembered my conversation the night before. I did not exactly muse over it, but because we had discussed the technique in such depth it was almost second nature for me to place the shot to her left and as she dived, her pony tail swinging, the ball skimmed under her body with an inch to spare. The grannies went wild and I rather uncharacteristically ran in a semi-circle towards the low warm winter sun with my arms outstretched mimicking a soaring eagle. It was a remarkable sensation. For a couple of seconds I was completely alone. I could feel the sun on my face and hear the applause of the spectators. I had done what I had for so long dreamed of doing. I had been fast, I had been skilful. I had made the difference against a team that had the beating of us. I had seen a fine keeper do her best but my best had been better. It had all felt so instinctive. I had felt, in short, like a real footballer.

My over-elaborate celebration stunned my team-mates and they did not rush to congratulate me. The half-time whistle blew and as we assembled for our team talk, Kev said gently: 'Great goal Ally. Now, it's 3–1, we are *in* this match.' Clearly the sensations that had overtaken me were personal and invisible to the others and, also, I recalled that whenever another girl had performed a solo miracle the response had been muted. For a short time I arrogantly assumed they were all in awe of my feat, but more likely those who had brought friends and family along were envious I had stolen the limelight and my obvious self-rapture was unbecoming. It remains my favourite of all the goals I have scored.

The following day I telephoned my date at his office. I wanted to tell him how I had put our theory into practice. I babbled a little and perhaps the bit about the sun in my face clouded the issue but then I was quiet to allow Adrian a few seconds to absorb the enormity of my achievement. And there was a pause. It was a rather longer one than I would have liked and he said: 'Er, that's nice Alyson.'

I wanted to scream 'What do mean "nice"? Where's your soul, did you leave it in the pudding I cooked you?' Instead I meekly responded, 'Well, I'll let you get back to work, I just thought, you know, as we'd talked about that way of scoring, you'd like to hear about my goal.' I was embarrassed. No doubt some agony aunt column on the do's and don'ts of dating would have said if you have just cooked dinner for a man you barely know, you wait for him to call you – and there are no extenuating circumstances. My call had not been a ruse to find out if he was 'still interested', as the magazines would put it, but now I felt pretty silly all the same. I won't see

ALYSON RUDD

him again, I thought to myself. That evening, as I arrived back home at gone 10 p.m. to my flat-mate's disgust, she sneered, 'Oh, and some bloke phoned. Is he the one you had round here?' Debbie was not dating anyone at all and had taken my recent behaviour badly, as though it had been written into our lease that if she had to stop in and binge on made-for-TV weepies then so had I.

Adrian had called to say he did after all appreciate the description of my goal, it had just been difficult for him to give it the attention it deserved while he was busy in his office. So we got married.

He watched me play for Orient three times. In all three games I was revoltingly pathetic. Afterwards he would say 'That Elaine's a good player' or 'what's your left full-back called, she's excellent'. I would be miserable for days and in the middle of *Coronation Street* would blurt out 'I'm good really, sometimes I'm really good.'

'Yes, dear.'

CHAPTER THIRTEEN

the awards ceremony

Karen and Kev had a housewarming party for the football team. I felt old. There was a lot of gossip and giggling about ex-players or old school friends I had never met. Only Kev was interested in talking about how bad Spurs were, a favourite topic of mine, but obviously I could not stand and chat to the only man in the house all night. Kev was so comfortable with it all. How many other men could have been host to an all-female party with their fiancée and her team-mates present without being lecherous, bored or embarrassed.

When he gave us pre-match team talks he never timed it wrong. He never barged in when we were half-dressed, he never made us feel uncomfortable and in turn we gave him the respect he deserved. It helped that he had a fiancée and we knew her. It meant there was no subtle question mark over any possible ulterior motive. Doubt did hang over Yvonne's brother's motives, however. He would turn up to give her a lift home and then turn up to watch the game and before long was a sort of unofficial assistant manager.

I thought he was probably bored by what a normal Sunday held for him and just wanted to feel involved and important. He was pleasant, had a few useful tips about tactics and gave vocal and much needed support from the touchline. But the rest of the girls decided he was simply excited at the prospect of being so close to a room heaving with perspiring young women in sports bras. One Christmas he bought each of us a red rose and the team sniggered what a dirty old man he was. It was an inappropriate gesture, certainly, but I felt sorry for him, not the least bit threatened. When Kev announced he would be retiring at the end of the season, Yvonne's brother wanted to step into his shoes, but the girls were having none of it.

No, the team wanted men who were married to or dating team members, not single brothers. This was patently unfair but I could understand the logic. If a man has his woman by his side he will not stoop to lechery or favouritism based on firmness of bottom. I had only been seeing Adrian a few months when they started asking if he would be our manager. I could not think of anything worse. Imagine if he dropped me from the team or made me captain. No matter what happened I would never be comfortable about it. Fortunately he had seen me dash out of my flat at nine on a Sunday morning to make a game the other side of London and said it all looked like too much hard work.

Elaine's brother had a six-week stint at the job but only because he was Amanda's boyfriend. I never found out if Amanda dated him because he was manager or if he dated her so he could become manager but their relationship only lasted while he was in charge.

Kev bowed out on the night of our end-of-season awards ceremony. I had bought an engraved trophy on behalf of his grateful team but two days before the bash my doctor told me to go to bed for four days with bronchitis. I liked this doctor very much. He was a total quack but I appreciated his completely empty and elegantly decorated waiting room and half expected a bill in the post so attentive were his receptionist and his good self. I never once saw another patient at his surgery but quite liked the fact he took my cough to be sufficiently serious for a sudden break from work. But could I really miss work yet travel to east London feeling bronchial and a shirker, just for a football bash? It was not that I minded the incongruity but I felt deep, deep, down that I would be attending for self-centred reasons; Rachel had said I had to go, because I had Kev's trophy, but there was a smirk in her voice that implied there was another reason. She was hinting I had won an award.

I really hoped that I had, but it seemed unlikely. Two awards were on offer. Players' Player, where the team votes, and Player of the Season which is in the gift of the manager. I was not popular enough to win the former and I did not think Kev would want to give an award to a player who was at best a maverick. I had had my midfield-general moments, but I had also had far too many Matthew Le Tissier ones and in my team, being called a Le Tiss was not complimentary.

Of course I attended, and because I had been presented with a mild health dilemma, the whole event felt worrisome and I silently scolded myself for wondering if Rachel's hints were fair or foul. All the club's various team members were there. The disco was too loud and the room was too small but there was a lively buzz and a bizarre female-to-male ratio of 70:1. Elaine told me I must have won the Players' Player award because everyone she had spoken to had voted for me and so had she. I was shaken to the core by this remarkable news and gazed in a crazed benign fashion at my fellow players like Sally Field on Oscar night.

Kev stood up and took the microphone. He emotionally bade farewell and said how much he had enjoyed being our manager and we whistled and hooted our thanks. Then he announced the first award. 'Players' Player is,' he paused 'Elaine Wright.' I felt myself flush. I was cross with myself for feeling a reaction and that made it worse. I had voted for Elaine and was pleased for her but I had somewhere in that part of the body which houses hope and vanity laid out a shelf just for this trophy. Elaine gave me a bold, pleased and knowing stare. 'God,' I thought, 'they're all in on it and I wasn't even close to winning.' Then Kev started describing the woman who was Player of the Season. I cannot remember what he said beyond the fact it was extremely generous and fine praise encompassing commitment and goalscoring prowess. 'So I am pleased to announce that in my view the outstanding player this season was Alyson Rudd.' I felt myself flush a far deeper red this time. The applause was loud. This was fantastic. Only. Only, wasn't the better award the one delivered by your peers?

I realised I was actually feeling, not delight, not surprise, but relief. Relief that whenever I had driven home, the windows down, after a game singing along raucously to U2 and not caring who heard because I had scored, because I had made the goal, I had not been deluding myself. I had won something that proved that, although very few people had actually ever watched me play well, I often did when no one was looking.

Rachel, meanwhile, took me to one side. She had a

secret and was not one for keeping them to herself. 'I had to sacrifice my principles for that award,' she said, knowing full well I would stare at her in horror and ask, 'What do you mean?' I had, in fact, won the Players' Player award by one vote. When she had told Kev this he had said he wanted to give me the other prize. 'Obviously,' said Rachel, 'you couldn't win them both so I changed my vote.' Reaction One: Why couldn't I win them both? Why not? Why not? Reaction Two: Why couldn't Kev change his mind instead of Rachel? Reaction Three: Shucks, what a wonderful team I play for. Just as Reaction Three was settling in Beth the boss announced that I was about to give a speech on behalf of my team thanking Kev for his services. My jaw sagged. 'What speech? I'm not giving a speech,' I told Rachel. 'Yes,' she smiled, knowing full well I could hardly refuse, 'you are.'

I took hold of the mike and unfortunately my 'I love you all' frame of mind strangled the 'I'm not prepared for this' shyness and I babbled. But I just made it through and gave Kev his trophy and he seemed pleased and no one teased me about the babbling. What a great bunch of girls.

With the exception of me. I proceeded to spend an unwholesome and wholly reprehensible 24 hours wondering who had not voted for me and why. This is how despots become despots. They win power but in winning know they could have lost. They remember there was opposition and they need to know who opposed them. If the majority wants me, thinks the despot, then the minority are driven by dastardly motives and they have to be destroyed. Fortunately, I soon stopped thinking about it and instead settled on genuine gratitude. All the same I am clearly allergic to awards and ought to have a card in my wallet informing any stranger who may find me wandering the streets in a daze that any plinth in my possession should be instantly removed and hidden from my view. For the prize also resulted in me subjecting my park boys to various conversations about my 'football career'. Should I move on, join a better team, or remain a big fish in a small pond? I recoil just from the memory. I must have believed that just because you win a prize you are a better player for it. I was also trying to tell the lads that although I may not often appear a good player, I obviously must be because I had won something.

Karen and Kev got married. Karen wanted the team to line up outside the church in full kit. This was something I would have done willingly and considered extremely amusing had I been 16 but I felt far too old to be hanging around churchyards in white shorts and red football socks. Still, I did it, out of loyalty to the newlyweds and because I respected Karen's desire to make football an important part of her big day. Needless to say all the elderly aunts and uncles found it hilarious in a risqué sort of way and I kept being nudged and asked whether I was cold. We assembled for a team photo of the bride and the Orient girls and that was that.

There is an automatic mechanism triggered by putting on a full football kit which leaves you feeling peculiar if you do not play. My fingers and toes tingled with blocked adrenaline, and although there was the wedding disco at which to unwind, it hardly helped. Only once before had the full kit gone on only for no football to be played. Greg, who else?, had organised a game on Hackney Marshes. I was itching to play, and arrived early but only three other members of the park boys were there, let alone any member of Greg's opposition. We spent an hour, growing increasingly annoyed, searching for them and then, reluctantly gave up. My anger and frustration was out of all proportion to the event, but when I acknowledged this I just became even more angry. Greg had, it turned out, given different instructions to everyone. Times, pitch numbers, pitch location, everything. We never stood a chance. I blanked him for a month.

Rachel was much better. Rachel was an expert organiser and after we had suffered numerous false starts with different trial managers, she took charge of Orient's Casuals. The first item on her agenda was to ditch the name. We wanted to win, we were not casual about that, so why give the impression we did not care? There was a poll on what our new name should be and the tremendously imaginative women of East London came up with Leyton Orient IVs. I meekly suggested that this was, if anything, worse. If you drew Manchester United IIs in the FA Cup you might be slightly worried, if you drew Manchester United IIIs you would be pleased but if you drew Manchester United IVs you would be hysterical. So what impact was Leyton Orient Ladies IVs likely to have? We knew we were not as bad as we sounded, but no one else would.

I was mistaken, slightly. An official title gave us more clout within the club and often our opponents were impressed that we were part of so grand an organisation that it could assemble four separate teams. But they were just as likely to feel insulted and I lost count of how many defenders tried to stare me out with a superior lift of the eyebrow.

We were an odd team. We varied in age, ability, education and attitude and usually faced teams that were homogeneous. They would be all tall former netball players from a single college or all from a police academy, or all tough cast-offs from another club. Most, although not all, of our victories were due more to the opposition's dismal organisation than any great tactical acumen of our own. Some teams were playing by numbers. They had started from scratch, had not watched any football, and were as unfamiliar with its workings as your grannie is with the internet.

The evil streak in me liked playing against these teams. I would receive the ball and note the panic in the eyes of the nearest defender. At such moments I could not help but draw a comparison with my games with men. I never approach a male defender with confidence that borders on arrogance, never. Yet here I was full of certainty that an eternity separated my ability from that of the startled female full-back.

Such teams always had a loud and despairing captain. Sometimes she could play, sometimes she was as bad as the rest, but she never gave up. In one game one such captain began by cajoling her players, encouraging them, praising anything that looked remotely useful. As one goal was conceded after another she then started to scream at them to concentrate. She tried to kick every ball and when she could not do that she did it vicariously, almost to the point of telling a team-mate how to perform the kicking movement. Her efforts were in vain and toward the end of the match she just kept muttering 'Oh for Christ's sake'.

I pitied them then. Presumably they had been mooching around the college coffee bar and thought it would be a laugh to try out a man's game. They were probably encouraged by the university, given a kit, a pitch and maybe even some funding, but then five minutes before their first competitive game the captain overhears one defender turn to another and ask, 'Have you heard about this offside thing?'

When Mark had been our coach he had paused during a training session and surveyed the motley bunch of women he was charged with turning into an unbeatable force. He had just mentioned offside and it had occurred to him that maybe women would not know what that meant.

'You know about offside, don't you? If anyone wants me to explain it just shout now.' There was a long silence and he looked relieved. Then Ann said 'Well I wouldn't mind hearing it explained properly.' Mark looked around suspiciously. 'You're not winding me up, right?' He then proceeded to make the whole offside rule sound as complicated as it was ever likely to get. Or maybe that was my personal interpretation. If you know about offside it always sounds incredibly awkward when anyone tries to explain it. It is something you feel, something you understand without analysing it. I only ever tried to explain it to someone who knew nothing about it the once. I was trying to prepare Caroline for her trip to see Atletico Madrid and, although I knew she did not really care if she died not knowing how important the word 'level' was, I persevered. It was when I started using the salt and pepper pots and drew a diagram that she averted her head slightly as if I was a grubby stranger with halitosis asking for directions to the red light district.

On a recent radio sports quiz show married couples were invited to participate and as a tie-breaker the host asked each girl to define offside. I am sure both had at least a vague idea of what it meant but it is quite possibly the most difficult rule from any walk of life to describe without preparation.

Once I was clean through and the referee whistled. 'What was that for ref?' I asked. 'You were offside.' I had not been and I was incensed. 'Are you sure you know the rules ref, it's when the ball is played that matters you know?' He did not reply, and I huffed and puffed with indignation. But most of my team-mates did not mind if they were pulled up for being offside. I half suspected they thought it was a good thing because they had heard famous players being called offside on *Match of the Day*. Once, against a team of fledglings, one of their forwards was flagged offside and as she walked back down the pitch one of her mates said 'Oooo so who's offside then?' and she giggled and said 'I know'. Good grief!

It became, for about three-quarters of one season, a bit of an obsession for me. Instead of concentrating on my own game I would for ever be issuing warnings to my team-mates about their positioning. To spoil a build-up with offside was like having a beautiful watercolour ruined by a splash of nail varnish. I could feel my pulse bouncing against the veins in my neck as I howled at Maria to move up the pitch. Her instinct and that of any of us who had made a run only for the ball never to arrive or to put a shot wide was to loiter deep in the opposition's half. I had done this myself but it did not stop me nagging everyone else to wake up. Oh, and it hurt me more than it hurt them. To make yourself heard on a wind-blown pitch took effort. I had to lower my voice and try to summon sounds from my stomach otherwise I sounded like a chimpanzee denied the mango at feeding time.

Beyond the obsession with offside I had no desire to

boss the girls around. This was partly because I was tired of all the bullying I put in with the boys and I needed a break. But I also liked the lack of responsibility. I liked sitting on the bench in the changing room squeezed in between Jenny and Elaine and feeling part of a group, just part of the whole. I liked listening to instructions. We were soldiers preparing for battle, aware that we could be massacred but hopeful we would conquer.

I really did regard the opposition as the enemy. Sarah, one of our defenders, was an incredibly sweet girl with an extra soft voice, freckles and a weight problem. Sarah thought it proper to engage members of the opposition in polite conversation which wound me up. I thought it proper to give members of the opposition a quick steely stare and then proceed to ignore them. Only if we were losing really badly did I relent and share a joke with one of them. Sarah was the epitome of the type of player who is nervous about football but is spurred on by some obscure reasoning that it is her duty to play it. She was by default offered the position of right full-back and then that of right-sided central defender when we switched to the sweeper system. Very quickly Sarah decided she could not really play football, but if she worked hard at being a defender she might not let us down. Sarah could and would not play anywhere else other than on the right side of our defence. For her the game did not encompass a pitch, it encompassed a patch — her patch and she marshalled it with intensity. Her priority was to get rid of the ball. Often she would have time, so much time, to stop, look up and pass to a team-mate but that would have meant thinking about someone else's patch, so she opted for tapping the ball over the touchline. To a cynical male this would have summed up all that is wrong with women's football. A short dumpy girl stands stock still ten yards from the touchline and ten yards from her own penalty area. Her nearest team-mate is 15 yards away, the nearest opponent is 20 yards away. Various team-mates scream for the ball. She pauses. She could pass the ball down the line, she could square the ball to the closest defender, she could run forward with the ball at her feet or she could attempt a cross-field diagonal pass. What she does is gently side-foot the ball out of play. The moment is ruined, the character of soccer is briefly assassinated. She has taken safety-first to a ridiculous level and put her team under unnecessary pressure.

But there were many times when we were grateful to Sarah for her conservatism. Few forwards ever got past her and she was always first to any 50/50 ball in her allotment. When we were being slaughtered, Sarah was one of the few players to emerge with credit. So what if she apologised to the opponent after every tackle? By the end of her tenure Sarah was as reliable as defenders get.

CHAPTER FOURTEEN

bitchy boys and butch girls

I once crystallised the difference between male and female footballers as 'we bitch less, spit less and kiss less', mainly because it sounded good, but there is some truth in it. Women are bitchy when sure of their status, when it is the workers v the bosses or the neighbours v the new couple who have just moved into number 24 and chopped down the weeping willow. But in a football team there is no concrete foothold and that curbs a lot, but by no means all, of the bitching that may well be lurking just under the surface. There is an acknowledgement that while you might be dying to satirise Deidra's tight shorts and hairy legs, there is always a basic insecurity that prevents you in case the manager picks Deidra for the team and leaves you on the bench. Women have spent their childhood suffering the swings and roundabouts of who is in and who is out and by adulthood have learned to hold their tongues in case they back the wrong girl.

Men seem less and more sensitive. They are fairer in that they are less likely to pick on a physical defect, but oblivious to what the repercussions might be should they air what complaints they do have. During that hiatus when the ball is booted out of play and no one wants to be the one to go and fetch it, the men gather in small clusters to mutter misgivings about players they have identified as annoying. They do this under the guise of talking tactics but really it is first-class bitching. They cock their heads, smile sardonically and gaze with a superior expression at the butt of their clever put-downs. A few of our park regulars are terribly clever in a first-class honours, late-night discussion on Radio Four sort of way, and they have a habit of equating career with footballing ability. So, a player who is an author and professor of literature and has sat next to Melvyn Bragg is, automatically, someone who appreciates the artistry of soccer and likes to play the passing game. Conversely anyone who mends roofs or sells cars is fit, fast and strong, of course, but impervious to the whole concept of total football. With this as their perception of our soccer soirées, the intelligentsia have plenty to bitch about.

We all do it. If a player is unfriendly or odd we look less kindly upon his contribution to the match. During organised 11-a-side games, it is the least popular player who via the general mutterings, I realise I could have taken off. Usually I take myself off but afterwards someone would say that I should have stayed on, that Ray should have been substituted as he had not put in the work rate.

No one wanted Ray to be there. No one has owned up to me how Ray came to be a regular. Even Ray cannot provide an adequate explanation, but then Ray fails to provide an adequate explanation about anything. In the early days Ray was part of a double act with Stan. Stan was a quite abysmal player. He was tubby and smelly and unfit. 'Well, you played better than Stan,' someone would comment after one of my less impressive evenings. Ray and Stan bickered all game long unless they had fallen out so badly that they could not bear to look at each other. Once one of our gang arrived with Stan having bumped into him on the bus and he could not shake off the glazed expression, that was a direct consequence of this chance encounter, for several weeks.

Stan whined and lived with his parents but was good at heart. No one paused to mourn his sudden disappearance from Regent's Park, however. Ray still turns up from time to time but is gradually reinventing himself. He is a more consistent player and can, on his day, be almost a pleasure to play with. His monologues are shorter now and less embarrassing, conspiracy theories having supplanted romantic melodrama.

'So, how are the wedding arrangements going, Ray?'

'Oh the wedding's off. She had second thoughts. Actually I think she's going out with one of my friends now, I don't blame her of course, my work meant I hardly ever saw her . . .'

These days the conversation goes more like this: 'How's the new job going Ray?'

'Not too bad really. I was fired basically for doing my job too well but I have to get the paperwork together to prove it . . .'

Perhaps the problem is with us and not with Ray. Football is about football. We do not meet up because we are lonely. Football is not the excuse, it is the reason. So, if one of us is late, we just say 'ugh, traffic' or 'ugh, tube'. Ray on the other hand will fill you in on the junction number where the traffic jam started and what was on the radio and how heavy the rain was and that he now has a company car.

While we are waiting for the game to get underway,

there is conversation, of course, and it is wondrously condensed. Kier may have just made a new documentary for Radio Four and had a new baby but such topics are covered in under one minute. A tackle committed by Roy Keane and highlighted on *Sportsnight* will be discussed by us in the remaining four. There is consequently a vague uneasiness when we gather en masse in the pub. As small groups who knew each other before football we are fine, but when we mix properly there is initially a hang-over from our 'waiting-for-a-game-speak'. This dissipates as we first discuss the game we have just played and then assess how our various clubs are doing in the Premiership, First Division or Dr Martens League. Then it's a final gulp of the shandy – or in the case of Orrin his thirst-quenching Guinness with blackcurrant juice – and we disappear into the night to our other lives.

One evening someone made the mistake of wondering which Spice Girl was dating Manchester United's David Beckham. It was an understandable error; pictures of the Spice Girls were plastered over the wrapping of the crisps we had piled onto the middle of our table and we were talking about United. But he had unwittingly brought a non-soccer topic out into the open. I did not care one way or the other, but, out of impishness, I slowly went anti-clockwise around the table asking everyone in turn who was their favourite Spice Girl. There was an endearing level of sheepishness as they replied and a strange willingness to wait until asked before revealing their choice. Other conversations continued as I slowly turned from one chap to the next but I could see their eyes dart nervously as their turn approached.

Women do not react like this. On the whole they

would be less certain of their favourite in an all-male pop group but, if they were sure, would not care who knew about it. It altogether prompted me to wonder if men take these things too seriously, that they care about Posh, or Scary or whoever, or perhaps they would rather that their predilection for big breasts or brunettes was not public knowledge. Either way it was weird and I think I'll stick to asking them who their player of the season is in future.

I could be in a more privileged position than I realise. By being part of a man's team and therefore part of the man's drink afterwards, I have penetrated a culture that I ought not to know about. If I were by accident to be the only woman in the pub for an after-work drink the conversation would not have been too different from the one that would have taken place had there been several women present. It would have encompassed holiday plans, gripes with the boss, the price of flats in Putney. But, on their own after football, men do not talk about such things.

I know very little about many of the men I have met up with at least once a week over many years. And still I know that I know more than anybody else. Their lives outside of what we have just been doing for the past couple of hours do not seem relevant and I even think, 'Oh, you're being a bit effete aren't you,' if one of the guys should stray too far and for too long from matters football. I know more because, if it is just me and one of them, we have a nearly normal conversation and, being manager of our little forays into more competitive matches, I hear all the excuses.

'My son's ill.'

'I didn't know you had a little boy.'

'I have to be in court tomorrow.'

'I didn't know you were a solicitor.'

In some ways not knowing all this is preferable because football ought to be egalitarian. The least well educated among us might play the most intelligent football, the most depressed might jump the highest and roar the loudest after scoring, the most powerful might play the worst, the kindest might be the dirtiest. It is too much knowledge about their backgrounds that results in the bitching and then taints our view of what we see them do. We ought to revel more in the fact we are so disparate, in contrast to professional footballers who all seem the same.

The pros have an out-of-kit uniform of flash suit and waistcoat and gelled-back hair and little to say of any real interest. They are pleased they scored but more pleased that the team played well and won. They do not criticise other players and have no view on world politics. It is Stepford Soccer. And sometimes when I play alongside a man with real talent, real understanding, I wonder how much better top professional players would be if they did more with their lives, if they were never allowed to take football for granted. It is a bore, sometimes, leaving work early and then struggling against the traffic to make our appointment with football in the park but thousands do it, and while they play that is all that they are. It is an escapism into sport and an escape from everything else that defines them. For an hour and a half all that anyone cares about is whether they will make the tackle, or take a decent corner kick. After that they can go back to saving lives, dreaming up advertising slogans or delivering parcels but not before having a quick drink with people they would never normally meet up with were it not for football.

From a distance I bet we all look like out-of-work yobs

or work-shy students. Very few of us are, in spite of the fact that a game in Regent's Park, or any park, costs nothing. It does cost effort, though, and slobs and layabouts have that in short supply. We are not yobs, but we are snobs. It is the precise opposite with the women and the reason why I never really, truly integrated and neither did Lydia the lawyer, because we were too middle class. Not that Lydia and I became firm friends. I liked her but she found me deeply irritating.

Lydia was one of the few members of our team who would show her annoyance at being left on the bench. She was tall and fairly broad and had perhaps found her youth trying as she would have been less feminine than most. Sport was one area in which she could put her physique to good use, and so it must have been deeply frustrating for her to discover that her build was not considered a vital asset. My intelligentsia boys would have put her down as a brickie if they had watched her play. She stampeded through midfield without, it seemed, any intention whatsoever of passing the ball at any juncture. Yet she was highly intelligent and knew her football. She was just transformed, when she put her boots on, into an energetic simpleton.

Perhaps this is why we in Britain fawn after foreign players who opt to live and play here. There is something disquieting about a player with poise and skill and finesse opening his mouth only for banalities to fall out. At least foreigners sound interesting even if they are not. Sometimes it works the other way around and a tough, aggressive player will be thoughtful and be shown to possess gentle good humour when interviewed by Garth Crooks. But no one who has ever earned a living from the game can compare with our Gary in the park. Gary is short, sweet and generous. He is funny, good-natured and adores his kids. If you were to watch us playing you would immediately fasten onto Gary. He arrives in motorbike leathers and when he unzips them reveals a tweed three-piece suit and a carefully knotted, carefully chosen tie. These he takes off gingerly and folds extremely carefully. He then slowly puts on his kit. His football shirt is ironed, his socks look brand new, his boots glisten in the sunlight. The whole process can take 30 minutes.

'For Christ's sake Gary,' we used to shout, 'Get bloody changed.' But now we know there is no point. To hurry is not in his vocabulary. So, having seen Gary eventually put his kit on, the man and his dog transfixed at the side of our pitch wait to see what kind of dainty and pretentious football Gary will play. Gary, though, is an animal. He hurtles around the pitch, tackling with two feet, his studs gouging through your thigh. He is commanding in defence, terrier-like in midfield and useful up front. He is energetic and enthusiastic and immune to pain. He returned to the park after a motorbike accident three months before any normal human being would have braved his own kitchen and insisted he went in goal even while he wore a plaster cast on his arm. After bravely diving to save one of my more accurate and powerful shots, he grinned and said I should have aimed for his bad arm.

Quite what it would take to make him cross, apart from the obvious trick of staining his tie, I do not know. During a five-a-side game he hurt his back and we all selfishly let him be assisted to the changing rooms by a complete stranger. When I called, far too many days later, to see how he was he chuckled and said the good Samaritan had helped him take his clothes off so he could wash, and he had been a little worried that he was about to have an embarrassing shower scene encounter, but then when he had finished his shower the chap had disappeared along with his wallet and £150 in cash – but not, evidently, with his good humour.

After a game in the park where there are no showers, Gary reverses the process and slowly changes back into his suit, ensuring that his tie is straight. It is all far more mesmeric than watching Superman twirl around inside a phone box to emerge with red underpants and a cape. By a twist of fate, or was it because he always wore white and I never did, Gary and I were once on opposite sides for eight weeks running. After nipping the ball from under my feet, he would wink, before whizzing away, or chirrup 'better luck next time Ally'. But he also ladles out generous portions of praise and encouragement and, although some of the bitchy boys think he is just that bit too hard in the tackle, he is very nearly the perfect park player.

As I said, women spit less. Certainly, the girls deposit fewer globs of phlegm per match than the blokes on TV. But in the park there is also, surprisingly, very little spitting. I spit, but only because I watch far more football than is good for me, and when I play I am subconsciously trying to re-enact all I noticed in the last game I watched. In fact a good spit during a girls' match does wonders for that hard woman image I would sometimes like, but cannot possibly maintain without first shaving my head and breaking my nose.

In fact a near-perfect moment in a woman's game for me is when I am covered in mud and bruises, have just sent a winger into a somersault and with my back to the wind I confidently spit onto the grass. Psychoanalysis would have something to say about rejection of femininity but really it is just play-acting. There is a very strong link between the type of game I have watched immediately prior to playing and the way I play. If it has been a game low on skill and high on midfield oppression I run around hassling the opposition and cannot pass to save my life. If, on the other hand, the game was one dominated by a diminutive flair player, I turn all pretentious and start back-heeling and then stand with my hands on my hips if my visionary pass has been misunderstood.

We kiss less. We girls, we ruffle hair, slap shoulders, clench palms, but we don't kiss the goalscorer. In the park with the boys it takes a goal of some quite immense beauty to prompt any sort of physical contact whatsoever. Goals in the park are treated differently. You could run the full length of the pitch, riding every tackle, tricking your way past every challenge, then flick the ball into the air before volleying it under the keeper's flailing grasp, complete a full somersault by way of celebration and find that most of the team are busy fiddling with their laces.

CHAPTER FIFTEEN

vanity

I have noticed that professional players with long hair start out with it loose and then after a few months, tie it back. I have also noticed that female players with long hair never play with it loose. Here, it seems, being a woman has its advantages.

Women are practical, they have chores to do and have evolved a system where they save their hair for when they are off-duty, on the pull, gracing the arm of a new beau. No woman would even pause to think about letting her hair fall across her face as she trotted about a football field, no matter how alluring it may look. Women footballers scrape theirs back without a second thought. But men, men with long hair are different.

Men with long hair are aware of their image, they have paused to consider how much more handsome they appear if their face is framed this way or that. They kid themselves that their masculinity is not affected and to prove it believe they must wear their hair long when they play football. To tie it back would be to admit publicly that their hair is impractical and therefore the product of vanity. So they try to play the game with poor peripheral vision, they make mistakes and their manager says, 'Tie your bloody wig back'. We then see them trot out of the tunnel sporting the most ridiculous contraptions in order to see properly. It could be a bandanna, a pony tail loop, a head band or even a combed Alice band, but whatever it is they look strange and, barring any lucrative advertising deals with shampoo manufacturers, they suffer for a while before chopping all their locks off.

The most amusing sight of all is the player who opts for what in my childhood was called a 'half up, half down'. This comprises a section of hair pulled back into a pony tail, leaving the rest loose. It was my preferred hair style when I was eight for it was practical and still pretty and told the world, 'Look I have nice long hair but I can still ride my bike without the wind blowing my hair into my eyes.' The half up, half down is currently particularly popular among French international footballers.

The women's changing room is refreshingly free of vanity. The first time I changed alongside the Orient girls I was apprehensive but I need not have been. There was a 'girliness' to the whole procedure but in style as opposed to content. So, in the tone you expect a girl to say 'Oh what gorgeous lipstick, does it have matching varnish?' I was asked: 'What shin-pads are you wearing. Ooh Gary Lineker endorsed pads, where did you buy those?' There was none of the 'God, I look awful' angst that normally accompanies a gathering of undressing women. There is more attention to detail than that found among the men I play with. A discussion on what kind of studs to wear was taken seriously. One of us would jog around the pitch and report back, and if a girl had forgotten to bring alternative boots, there would be a short burst of anguish but no long-term moaning about it. Conversely, the boys are almost too shy to discuss the hardness of the pitch. They like to just get on with it, not talk about it. Only Frank and Gary ever suddenly leave the pitch to change boots. They can get away with this because Frank acts out the whole real footballer thing, right down to the way he rubs his hips and Gary is the obsessive/compulsive.

Team talks with the girls were more detailed, too. With the men a form of soccer shorthand suffices. To over-stress any point is regarded as effete and an insult. With the women, particularly my women, who had learned to play late in their lives, there was no shared experience, no football roots and so we had to talk the tactics through slowly. Sometimes Mark or Kev would refer to 'pushing up' or 'dropping deep' and I could see a quizzical look pierce the eyes of some of my team-mates, and if Mark or Kev saw it too, they would try to explain what they had in mind.

Once out on the pitch the differences faded. Captains, whether male or female snipe and growl and cheer and congratulate. Afterwards, though, while the men laugh it all off, the women brood. 'She can't talk to me like that, who the fuck does she think she is?'

Fans of women's football say it is enjoyable to watch because the emphasis is on skill and movement. It is slower than a men's game and simpler to read. The equivalent men's game contains more posturing, more long-range passes, more crosses into the penalty area and as a consequence the ball finds itself in the air for longer periods. A classic women's game has poise and intelligence.

Sometimes our team just clicked, everything slid into place as if by supernatural force, for there was rarely any indication during training it might be so. The most trying times for me were when the team played well but I played poorly. Everyone has games when their touch deserts them, when luck avoids them, but I really worried when I was rubbish. My head would begin to cloud and the game would appear murky and vague in outline. I would feel gawky, ungainly and unfit. My levels of self-consciousness would reach bursting point. When I played well I felt beautiful, elegant and athletic, but the bad days brought out acne, frizzed my hair and knobbled my knees. My confidence soared on the good days and I believed I was capable of anything. I even tried flicking the ball over my head ready to turn and spin on to it leaving the defender flummoxed and humiliated; it only partially came off. Even when the less ambitious tricks worked my team-mates failed to be astounded but nothing, not even collective sarcasm could stop me.

The joy of feeling good after all those years of feeling inadequate and out of place was just too delicious. After being out-muscled and out-run by the men, I was, suddenly, stronger and faster than most. To see the ball fall in the near distance, to see an opponent turn to race towards it, to know I was likely to reach the ball before her, such confidence turned my head. Most of my goals were the product of relative speed and a loose ball. A poor clearance by the keeper would leave me one-on-one with the defender and I would usually get there first. In training, my shots at goal were ordinary, if not deeply unimpressive, but in a match I was transformed. Adrenaline improved my accuracy and power. A real striker does not and should not think too hard about his or her shot. The instinct is everything and when on form my instincts were powerful. On a bad day

I pondered the shot, feared the repercussions of a mistake and inevitably scuffed the earth. I used to shout hearty abuse at professional players who missed from two yards but having done the same I am less outraged.

During one Orient match, and inevitably, Beth the boss was watching this one time, Elaine crossed from the right wing. The ball dipped into the penalty area and Marie launched her not inconsiderable frame toward it. Her header was greeted with squeals of delight, so rarely did one of us ever attempt to head the ball, but the ball hit the cross-bar and dropped right in front of me. I must have been a matter of feet from the goal-line but as I lunged forward the ball's trajectory changed. It was suddenly spinning away from me and my first inclination, to head the ball too, had to be dampened. I tried to chest the ball instead but it whizzed into the arms of the goalkeeper. From a distance this looked a terrible miss. Beth the boss muttered she thought I was better than that, and all the team's talk was of Elaine's fabulous cross, Marie's brave header and then a silent, accusing sidelong glance at me.

Only once, and that was in the park with the boys, did I let the stream of shoddy passes and shots that left my boots get the better of me. I stormed off saying, 'I'm too crap for this.' No one argued with me and the sensation that the lads were glad to be rid of such a grotesque liability completed a miserable evening.

If the whole Orient team performed badly I was less battered by the experience. There was a sort of camaraderie in defeat, we could all sigh as one and blame the pitch, the referee, our hangovers. It still felt good, to have run around for 90 minutes, trying to score, trying to hold the others at bay, and we always took something out of defeat, someone could be praised.

During a poor woman's match the ball is barely in play. All the players can do is hoof the ball into the woods or down the ditch and the referee tires of telling them that their throw-ins have been illegally taken. My team lost possession, on average, three times per match because of a badly taken throw-in. Referees in men's matches do not bother with such trifles but give them a bunch of women to control and their inner patronising voice informs them that women are novices and have to be berated for their mistakes.

I never knew where all our referees came from. It staggered me that there was a steady supply of men, and the very occasional woman, who were prepared to give up their Sunday afternoons to officiate a game as low on the rung of football's ladder as ours. Yet turn up they did and they took it so seriously. Prior to one cup match the referee knocked on the changing-room door and then when told he could enter did so bearing a very grave expression. He then lectured us on our duty as players, that he would not tolerate any bad language or anyone arguing with his decisions. He told us to take off all our jewellery, 'except wedding rings of course' and far from inducing a sense of honour, all he achieved was to make us feel like pros and aggressive ones at that. 'Bloody wanker,' said Carol after he left the room.

Generally though these referees simply could not accept that a woman can be violent. The most vicious and gratuitous tackle often went unpunished. The referee simply refused to believe his eyes. Blood could be dripping from a girl's knee as she appealed for a free kick following a nasty studs-up interception but the man in black would just smile and usher play on. That same official would then blow shrilly on his whistle to admonish one of us for having her shirt hanging outside her shorts. Very gradually, and without really openly acknowledging it, we became more violent because it paid off. Not only would many of the referees refuse to accept that a woman could be rough, they also turned a blind eye to cheating. Hand-balls were never penalised; the refusal to move the wall back at a free kick was judged not be intransigence but ignorance. Penalty kicks were occasionally awarded, however, since even the most sexist ref cannot resist the drama of a spot kick.

It was no coincidence that the one woman to referee our matches dished out yellow cards. I have never been booked and I wish that I could be. It is a sensation I think I ought to experience in order to justify my claim to be a footballer. Would I feel admonished, small and embarrassed, or aggrieved and brutal? As for being sent off, now that would be an experience. But I have never seen a woman shown the red card. If I had, I am certain the woman would have been ugly and butch. Referees are vulnerable when face-to-face with a pout, a pleading smile, pale blue eyes and a little, turned up, pixie nose.

And what about the men who play alongside the Astroturf Blonde? Are they influenced by the size of my thighs, the delicacy of my wrists, the colour of my teeth? I know what I think, but I am not so sure I am right to think it. There is no sexual chemistry on a football pitch, there is no time for that. The football is everything. No one has forced us to play, we want to be there, we need to be there. The football is our fantasy, not whether or not one of the lads scores with a girl who might be playing. Yet sometimes there is a glance exchanged that carries more than a glance between two men. I interpret this as fraternal encouragement or harmless and tongue-in-cheek flirtation. Just occasionally, if my husband is on my team, I frown if he has not passed to me for a while but I would hate it should he pass to me too often. After all how can there be sexual chemistry when, since the arrival of Adrian, first as my boyfriend and then my husband, there has been no change in the attitude of my male team-mates. I was Ally and I still am. They know I am female, and have and always will give me that little bit of extra praise or encouragement, but I have been around them for so long I have ceased, if it was ever there, to inspire a crumb of ardour.

I could be wrong. It may simply be that attraction exists but who among them would be fool enough or vain enough to assume they could be special. Perhaps they regard themselves as a single male entity, sufficiently magnanimous to permit a woman to play and sufficiently modest to assume that the woman cannot really tell them apart. Only once has one among them dared to attempt a seduction. It failed, as I think he knew it would, for his hands trembled as they reached for my modest bosom and my laughter brought relief, not humiliation. I confided the incident to one other in the park team and he was as angry as a big brother in a musical set at the turn of the century and wanted to punch the offender on the nose. But I placated him and we all carried on playing as normal.

I do not feel particularly attractive when I play anyway. Only when I have one of my special games do I feel I might be the most wondrous woman in the world and then perhaps there is attraction. It is an attraction borne of performing admirably rather than of pretty curls and a small waist. Only after one of my special games does my husband kiss me. I think I am suddenly more attractive to him, too, for he never kisses me in public otherwise. I do not mind the androgyny of the football in the park. After all, I want to be a footballer, not a siren and if I was devastatingly gorgeous my presence might have been less acceptable to the men who taught me to play in the first place. When I play I dream only that all anyone will see is skill or pace or vision. When I was mistaken for a man, I was genuinely, if absurdly, pleased as punch.

In any case I was well prepared for the lack of sexual interest my footballing career would engender. No one ever chats me up or ever has. After an evening surrounded by men at some corporate hospitality event I wondered just how unattractive I must be. My friend Sue had suffered a similar event and been inundated with indecent proposals plus a couple of honourable ones. I, on the other hand, swim through such evenings without so much as a ripple of a chat-up. 'Has anyone ever told you your eyes are painfully beautiful?' No, they have not. I have been spared all the corny one-liners, all the heavy breathing, all the suggestive remarks. I am glad, of course, but the inescapable conclusion was that I am deeply unimpressive to members of the opposite sex.

I mentioned this to Dominic in a sad flurry of self-loathing. Dominic has known me a long time. He smiled and thought for a moment whether the knowledge he possessed should be shared. At length he said that many men had confided in him that they thought I was desirable, but they were scared of letting me know about it. 'You put them off,' he told me. 'Your whole manner says don't flirt with me.' Since then I have been armed with this jewel of a fact and it has seen me through many a bad hair day. It has also protected me against concern that, being involved in such a male pursuit as football, I may be asking for trouble. I am, after all, just a footballer. And, quite rightly, only when my football is worthy do I introduce a sexual frisson into proceedings.

Among the women looks mattered not one jot. There were two sorts of woman, the sort that had a boyfriend and the sort that did not. There were continuous dark mutterings about who was lesbian, who might be a lesbian. There was genuine anger among some of the girls that their football club was being abused. They hated it when teased at college or work that if they played football they must be gay. They took their indignation out on those who were gay. Remarks went thus, 'She should be chucked out the club, we don't want dykes here.' 'I heard off Jane that Moira was in the bedroom and in bed with that traffic warden woman – in her house, the cheek, it's disgusting.'

Girls who were considered dykes were openly snubbed. I had heard my neighbours in Walthamstow emit racist noises about West Indians and Pakistanis and learned enough about Hitler at school but this was the first time I had encountered sexual fascism. It was blind, unadulterated disgust. Or at least those who gossiped about the dykes felt they had to project blind, unadulterated disgust. To suggest all women had every right to live as they pleased would be to admit possessing lustful thoughts towards every girl in the shower. At one point I was told that only the gay girls took showers, at another that all policewomen were lesbians. It was extremely silly. One girl was being criticised for being a poor passer of the ball, for failing to turn up to training and as her accuser sensed no one was much bothered she triumphantly announced that this girl was also a dyke.

The purges seemed to peter out after my first year with Orient. This coincided with various administrative changes within the club, which I took little notice of, but the gossip said that someone important was having an affair with someone else important and the accounts at the club had been neglected. It took the close season to sort out but Orient emerged a stronger and better run outfit.

As the seasons passed so did the personnel. There were the stalwarts but new players joined and some were already good, others were promising. We began to be more selective, as the club was buckling under the weight of new members. Our team lost its character and was much like the others at Orient. The emphasis was on winning, not on giving slightly older women a chance.

To my horror another Alison joined. I whittered incessantly like a canary with its cage curtain whipped away that this was an impossible state of affairs unless my team-mates strictly adhered to the 'Ally' nickname. Sometimes they forgot, sometimes they called Alison, 'Ali' and I would whinge on and on that such errors could lose us the match on Sunday. My suggestion that we re-name Alison as Geraldine or Julie was greeted with puzzlement and Alison looked horrified. What made it worse was that Alison was thin, thinner than I, and fast too. They put her on the right-wing for a while and plonked me briefly on the left. As I am right-footed I regarded this as an insult and during one half-time team talk I proclaimed that the reason we were losing was that I was being played out of position.

This was self-centred nonsense which my team more or less put up with. I blamed other things, not least the arrival of another Alison, but the truth was, I had stalled and younger women were catching up with me.

CHAPTER SIXTEEN

the biggest match of all

I have never played in front of 70,000 spectators. That probably comes as something of a surprise and a disappointment. Perceptive readers may even have guessed that the denouement of *Astroturf Blonde* would be that I successfully disguised myself as a man and scored the winning goal in the 1998 FA Cup final. No, the ending is far more exciting than that. But the big match in my career has to be the first, and most likely the last, time I played in a league stadium.

Rachel, as was her wont, mentioned the possibility in passing. Rachel liked to season dull conversation with sprinklings of tasty gossip and monumental news. 'I can't say any more just yet,' she said, immediately adding 'but we might be able to play at Brisbane Road.' I pleaded, begged, cajoled for more information and in order to remain sane persuaded myself it was just talk. No way would Leyton Orient just lend us their stadium. Does the Queen let the lads down the local boozer play cricket on her lawn? Does the National Gallery lend paintings to anyone who says pretty please?

To anyone who thinks Brisbane Road is more on a par with a minor duchess and the Oswestry Lending Library, think again. Leyton Orient's ground has won awards for having the best pitch in the country. The club's groundsman was for ever being asked to switch to a top club. To play at Brisbane Road was a big deal.

My cynicism as to the likelihood that I would, was based upon my recent dealings with Wembley Stadium. Depressed about the approach of my 30th birthday I concluded that the only way to avert months of angst was to celebrate in some style and that meant playing a match at Wembley. I aired the proposition after a game in Regent's Park with the lads and they were keen on the idea too. After much fantasising disguised as planning, I resolved to sort it out. I telephoned the stadium and asked to speak to whoever organised leasing it out. This I did in all seriousness. This was no prank, no wind-up.

'Ah, yes good morning I understand you are in charge of hiring out Wembley?' The man on the other end of the phone was courteous and keen. 'How much do you charge for, say, 90 minutes on the pitch and the use of the changing rooms?' He wanted to know when. 'Obviously,' I said, 'only when you've got a gap, I wouldn't want to play there the night before an international.' He wanted to know what the occasion was and when I told him it was for my birthday, he snorted derisively. 'We don't hire it out for birthdays, this is the national stadium, it would denigrate its status. If I let you play here where would it end?' I asked him if anyone else had asked to play there for their birthday and he conceded that no they had not. 'Well then,' I said, 'why not let us play and I promise we won't tell anyone. Surely it is better to have the stadium in use and earning money than standing idle.' Suddenly his attitude changed. 'I don't think you could afford it,' he said.

'I might,' I said trying to sound titled and independently wealthy.

'How much would you charge?' The cost, he said, would be £100,000. 'That's quite a lot,' I replied trying to sound only slightly nonplussed rather than completely gobsmacked. 'If you could get 2000 friends to watch paying £50 each you could do it,' he offered. So much for denigrating Wembley's status. Everything has its price.

Rachel had not been leading us down the garden path. A date was fixed in May. Our opposition was Clapton Orient Ladies. I had never heard of them but I hardly cared about that. The reason we were allowed to play at Brisbane Road was complicated. The league club were very community conscious. They had to be. Many of their potential supporters were Asian, black or female and not interested in Orient or any other team. Everyone else headed off to Upton Park. For reasons I neither knew nor cared about, the club had helped to set up Clapton Orient. The game was for them, not us. We were chosen by Clapton to be their opponents for this prestigious occasion.

'But why us?' I asked. It seemed fishily fortuitous. Beth the boss explained that we had at some point lent Clapton players when they were establishing themselves and this was their way of saying thank you. 'I thought we didn't lend teams players, they just got poached,' I said.

'No, no you've got that all wrong,' said Rachel, concerned that the bar was bugged and the opportunity of a lifetime was about to pass us by. To be honest I did not care if Clapton Orient's women were behind a series of gruesome gangland killings, I just wanted to play in the match.

I was so excited, excited in that childlike way where there is nothing but wonderfulness to look forward to.

I was so excited that I mentioned the game to *The Times*. To my astonishment they were excited too. They commissioned a piece about the match and added, as if as an afterthought, that they would send a photographer to Brisbane Road. This lent whopping great heart murmurs to already worrying palpitations. Under no circumstances must my team-mates find out about this, I thought.

I arrived early on the evening of the match. So, independently, did the rest. We walked slowly towards the floodlights. They would not be needed but that they existed was breathlessly awesome. Girls who had hitherto seemed hard as nails, as capable of emotion as a dozing Vulcan or Alan Shearer, were twittering in anticipation. We had suffered many changing-room moods and not always been as all for one and one for all as we should, but in the changing room that night we were united. My suggestion that, as this was our Wembley, we should stroll about the pitch before we put on our kits, was not greeted with the 'you can be so pretentious' glares that I half expected.

The pitch was every bit as lovely as I had hoped. The grass was as smooth as felt and rose at the centre circle. The goalposts were firm and solid, their angles were perfect. They did not creak when I leant against them and there was no graffiti, no chunks of paint flaking free. And the nets billowed a brilliant white and had not been darned. The stands were dilapidated but as I had never before played on a pitch that had terracing, they seemed at that moment to be monumental.

Then I spied Mark, *The Times'* photographer. When the paper had told me Mark would take the pictures I had been grateful because I had met him before and would therefore be able to spot him easily. That had been a ridiculous response. How many other professional sports photographers with zoom lenses the size of a bicycle were there likely to be attending this fixture? I hurried over to him. He seemed less amused by the assignment than I feared and I had to quell the tingling sensation of pride that was starting to munch at my brain.

'Mark, Mark, psst. I can't talk long. Do not tell anyone, and I mean anyone, that you're here to take pictures of me and do not take pictures of me looking stupid.' With that I was gone leaving Mark to wonder what had happened to the girl he had had such a pleasant chat to only three weeks previously on a photo shoot in Nottingham.

As we waited for kick-off I could feel the oxygen oozing out of my head. It tends to do that when I am very nervous. When I was 16 I appeared as team captain on a TV schools quiz and the minute the director became serious and counted in the filming I went deaf, dumb and blind. I could not hear any of the first few questions and had no idea how long the state of paralysis would last. All I could think was 'I'm supposed to buzz and answer, buzz and answer.' Eventually my right forefinger pressed down and the quiz-master briskly said my name. I had not recovered sufficient composure actually to know the answer or to even know that I did not know it and so I said something stupid like 'Buck Rogers'. Well, that is precisely what I said in fact, and then I flung up my arms and said 'Oh, didn't mean to say that.' And when the quiz-master gave the correct answer, he smirked at the camera and then me and asked, 'Is that what you meant to say?' and I muttered in despair, 'No, I was thinking of something completely different and just as completely wrong,' when

I knew that on other quiz shows contestants just said yes Mike or no Des.

Here it was happening again. Suddenly the pitch seemed too large, the ball too small, my legs too wooden, my understanding of the game's few rules too Neanderthal. I did not know where to be, who to shout to. The grass seemed to be about to swallow me up. Then I heard the supporters. There is something disconcerting I am sure about the wall of sound that greets players when they have 40,000 people all screeching and singing and blaspheming at the same time, but it was equally disconcerting to hear the chiffon curtain of sound of 30 or so supporters all living it up in what usually passes as the directors' box. How their voices carried. I could hear every word, even the asides that were not meant as supporter chants. I could also make out who said every word. I had enticed three supporters, Sheffield John, Brummie John and Adrian, and had been grateful for their interest. Now I wished they would shut up. As we had trotted out of the changing rooms and through the tunnel towards the pitch, Mark had suddenly appeared above us and had nearly hit me on the head with his Pentax so keen was he on his whites-of-the-eyes approach. Rachel had turned to me and asked if I knew who he was.

'He looks quite professional doesn't he?'

'He's probably a boyfriend of one of the Clapton girls,' I lied.

That had satisfied Rachel then but now Mark was following me about. As I ran down the right flank I heard a shutter clicking and, startled, I realised how close Mark was. 'Go away' I muttered. He didn't. I carried on running and was passed the ball. The goal-line beckoned. I would normally have stopped, turned to face away from the goal to see who was free and then passed, or possibly cut into the penalty area. But nothing was normal in that match. I had friends in the stand and a lens trained on my every movement. A professional player, or a half-decent any sort of player would cross first time without breaking their run and deliver a looping and dangerous ball into the heart of the six-yard box. I wanted to do the same. I had after all been practising such a delivery, or at least had tried it out a couple of times after a picnic with Adrian. As I lifted my right foot the camera went 'Shuutticca, shuutticca' and the ball sliced off my boot and bounced pathetically into the empty stand behind the goal. Elaine applauded the effort, perhaps understanding why I had tried something she had never seen me do before, but I hung my head in shame. I had no right to waste possession on a vainglorious whim.

I had one chance to make amends. The ball was driven low across the face of the Clapton area and in true striker's fashion I slid in hoping to reach it before my marker. I did, but the ball zipped a yard the wrong side of the upright. I could hear the boys moan the famous football supporters' lament, 'Yeeeessssnoooaahh.'

At half time we were a goal down. The chirruping good humour of the changing room before kick-off had been replaced by a querulous air as Rachel announced substitutions had to be made. I could not bear to look at her. 'Please God not me.' I could tell she was considering me. I was not having one of my better games but, she said later, I had it in me to do something to turn the game in our favour so she stuck with me. There was much furrowing of brows, of failure to make eye contact and Amanda stormed off in a self-contained frenzy. Only Elaine could afford to gaze about the room in frank openness. But one of the mums had brought oranges and we cheered up and improved enormously. Some of our football really was splendid free-flowing intelligent stuff and I felt proud to be part of the concerted and delight-to-behold effort.

We lost 2–0. It was that goalkeeper, the one I had beaten in the sunshine, but she was even better now at her new club. And they possessed a truly gifted midfielder who glided with imperious ease through the centre of the pitch. We were later told she was an ex-professional ballerina. We shook hands and lapped up the applause from the directors' box. Rachel said, 'That photographer was pretty interested in you.' But she left it at that. We gabbled incessantly about how well we had played and marvelled at the enormous shower area. Only about two or three of us usually bothered to shower after games. They are normally without warm water, full of adolescent boys or just plain disgusting. These were fairly antiquated, but reliable and hot, and both the novelty of using professional facilities and an urge to bond after our experience meant we all rushed about like under-fives at a paddling pool party. I offered my Chanel soap, dug out especially for the occasion, to anyone who needed it, and again the 'pretentious git' response was notably absent. We would have been far more delirious had we won but it really mattered that we had played well.

At the next training session most of the team were huddled around a photocopied piece of *The Times*. Rachel's father-in-law or cousin or whoever had seen my article about the game in the paper and sent her a copy. The feature had been accompanied by a photograph of me looking for all the world as if I was jogging alone on the Yorkshire moors rather than participating in a team sport involving 21 other women. My team-mates' first gripe was that they were not in the picture. 'There were loads of group photos taken, so why didn't they print one of them?' they moaned. Their second gripe was my reference to the shot I pulled wide as being our best chance. There was much humphing and tutting and glowering and a small chasm opened up. They thought it was all far too wordy and pretentious. I was not sure how to respond. I had nothing to apologise for, the piece was after all a fine advertisement for our club and for women's football, but just the fact that I was in a position to write about our shared experience in a national paper made them suspicious, the way intelligence officers in the Second World War grew suspicious of a supposed trusty agent who knew far too much about Bavarian sausages. I think they felt, if not thought, that I was using them, patronising them. Does Steve McManaman get that sort of treatment when he writes about his performances in *The Times*? Almost certainly.

It is all part of New Football to be literate or discursive about the game. If you throw in the word 'philosophy' you are an esteemed and intelligent manager, if you throw in the word 'rehabilitation' you are the model footballer. But for many of those who play the game at whatever level, anything written that seeks to go beyond, 'Smith was fantastic and deserved the hat-trick which took Rovers to the top of the table' is superfluous stuff and nonsense. But then the fancy stuff is not written for them is it? It is written for the millions who wanted to play at Wembley but lacked the talent or the muscle or the character to turn their backs on a secure job. For them football is art, a dream, passion and devotion, a pastime. I become watery eyed over soccer because I have elevated its status. Just occasionally I think about war and famine and fear that my priorities are wrong. The world needs people to care about starvation and corruption not strike rates and formations but I only tried to get clear in my mind what the divisions were in the former Yugoslavia when I had to preview a match being held in Belgrade.

The mistrust on the faces of my team-mates as they read my account of our big night reminded me that all I wanted to do was play football, not win their hearts. In that respect I was even more peculiar than they thought. If there is one big difference between men who play football and women who play it, it is that women join clubs for the chance to meet people as much as to play a sport they either love or quite like or even mistrust. When a bloke asks for a game, he wants a game, not a trendy substitute for a Tupperware party. Now that I have to keep my playing time down to one match a week with the lads, I do not keep in touch with a single one of the Orient girls. Who can blame me?

And who can blame them?

CHAPTER SEVENTEEN

glamour, obsession and Paul Ince

The more football I played, the more football-obsessed I became. Not a day passed when football did not dominate it. Now that football is also my legitimate job, there is more order and reason, but before I discovered a way of earning my living from the sport, its domination was possibly slightly unhealthy.

A typical week passed thus.

Sunday: I played in a league match for Leyton Orient Ladies.

Monday: I bored everyone with tales of my exploits the previous day and then went home and watched football on satellite TV.

Tuesday: I trained with the women.

Wednesday: I went to a game.

Thursday: I played with the men and then rushed across London to train with the women.

Friday: Nothing to do.

Saturday: Went to a game.

That was the bare minimum, the back-drop for any kind of footballing activity I could worm my way into. I would press my office to enter competitions and before long we had our own strip fashioned after Barcelona's with our company logo subtly displayed where a badge should be. In the meantime I wrote about the City and financial regulation. In many ways I was fortunate that I did because insurance and investment companies are so grossly male-dominated that when I started work in football I did not notice how few Laura Ashley dresses there were in the press room. I had long since lost count of the occasions I was invited to a City boardroom lunch only to find myself sat primly at a gleaming, long oak table sharing venison with twenty cigar-puffing executives.

'Well my dear. Do you realise you are the first female ever to have entered this room?'

They were strange times. I was a real oddity for these gentlemen but my very first experience set me up nicely to cope with it all. I was a cub reporter, learning the ropes across several financial titles, and was told to interview the chief executive of an American bank which was expanding its range of financial services in the UK. I was extremely nervous, believing that this powerful and successful businessman would feel affronted at my own youth and inexperience. But upon entering his plush office I noted that his body language was defensive and even over the introductions his voice trembled. The real give-away was the rivulet of perspiration running down his forehead. Did I then try to put him at ease, to strike up a gentle conversation before asking more serious questions? No, of course not. As luck would have it I had some personal experience of his company's services and was able to contradict one of his claims about his products, and in true obnoxious, keen young journalistic style I hammered away at the discrepancy. His bank never contacted my magazine again, at least not while I was there. I am not even sure the bank exists now.

That episode gave me a sense of the power of the press which was bolstered as I rose to the position of first news editor and then editor and was wined and dined and generally ingratiated upon. Lunching was hard work. Every now and again I would meet someone who was particularly intelligent or amusing and it would be a pleasure to discuss their business, but more often than not my hosts would be without humour, their accompanying public relations staff would be without intellect and my ambassadorial technique would be stretched to the limit. Often the only way I coped was by the adrenaline kick I received by not preparing for the lunch meeting. I had to ad-lib, think of questions on the spot, decide on an instant opinion. I was always aware that, had I been the same age and male, the lunch would have been more enjoyable for everyone. We could have swapped public school stories, been lewd, perhaps even talked about cricket. I did not want to be patronised and preferred not to discuss anything in a light-hearted way in case I confirmed their suspicion that I must be dumb because I was blonde. They probably had as dull a time as I did.

Very, very few of the executives and managers I met liked football. Very few knew what it was and would have been hard pressed to answer the question: who plays in red, at Highbury and their name begins with an 'A'? But during my stint in the financial world, there were threats to the establishment. New companies were being created that hoped to profit from the established competitors' complacency. These firms had younger and more dynamic staff at the helm and knew about and liked their football. What better way to ensure their products were written about than to invite that young football crazy writer to their box at Wembley for the FA Cup final?

Corporate hospitality at great sporting events is revolting. There is something obscene about sitting in a cosy room, glass separating you from the fans outside, with your goblet of wine hidden from their view by the cleverly positioned shelf under the window. I was uncomfortable, not just because I would have preferred to have been in the crowd and closer to the game I love, but because the attitude was one of indulgence. There was no real sense that anyone appreciated how fortunate they were to be there. Once I was a guest for lunch at a Test match at Lord's. I have never played cricket and cannot claim to understand it fully but I knew this was a great sporting occasion, a sell-out. Yet as lunch in the marquee progressed, I was perplexed by the lack of interest there was in the game. The TV monitors showed that the teams were back out on the field yet the men in suits were ordering extra coffee and brandy and snuggling down into their chairs. What was the point of them being there? They might as well have met up in a restaurant miles from St John's Wood. There were a few disapproving glances in my direction as I announced it would be a shame to miss any cricket but they missed out on a vibrant and fun afternoon in the sun.

At Wembley I hated the long drawn-out preamble of the lunch before kick-off, which made it more obvious that the match was the carrot and the stick was the corporate speak you had to endure over the beef wellington and claret. Then, when the game is underway you discover you are sat next to another guest who accepted the invitation out of politeness and curiosity having never been to a football match before and he is bored after five minutes.

'Do you know who all those players are? Gosh, you must be a real aficionado. Fancy another drink?'

I totally disapproved of the entire enterprise but when the final went to extra time and then with Manchester United and Crystal Palace locked at 3–3, the outcome was a replay, I immediately accepted the invitation to attend it. Later my colleagues just stared at me with annoyance and incredulity as I explained that it was my moral duty to see the match through to its conclusion and it would be rude to pass the invite to anyone else.

'Of course you were the one invited Alyson, you were there and they had to. They are probably hoping they won't have to put up with you again.' They were spot on. As we turned our chairs around to watch the replay, the managing director smiled and said, 'I hope you'll be a little less, er, enthusiastic, this time.'

I assumed that he was a United fan and had been put out by my support of the underdog and I thought no more about it, but that was not what he meant at all. A short while later my friend Dominic invited me to his company's box at White Hart Lane for a midweek game. I was there ostensibly as a journalist, but really because I had known Dominic since college. But it was a serious business for Dominic, he was entertaining important clients and his boss would be there.

'Try to behave, won't you, you know, in front of my boss.'

I assured him I would indeed behave impeccably and was polite and interesting over dinner and then nestled into the corner of the box to watch the match. Afterwards Dominic shook his head. 'I thought you weren't going to show me up,' he whispered. I was genuinely astonished. I thought it had all gone swimmingly. But unbeknown to me, as I had been wrapped up in the game, I had, I was told, sworn more or less continuously throughout the entire 90 minutes.

'No, I don't think so. I was trying hard to be good,' I said, genuinely confused.

'Oh, Alyson, you even said "Fucking stupid git" at one point.'

'Oh, that must have been when Liverpool went behind,' I said, baffled that I did not even know I had said it.

Poor old Dominic also had to suffer the embarrassment of watching me put my 'the way to handle a footballer theory' to the test. I maintained that fans and the media generally act as though they have the right to be on first name or nickname terms with footballers and so even the most famous are subjected to complete strangers saying, 'Hey, Gazza, can I have your autograph?' Therefore, I argued, the way to ensure attention from a famous player, was to be incredibly formal.

'Watch this.' I instructed Dominic, as Paul Gascoigne walked past us surrounded by an entourage of minders. I strolled confidently towards the man who was then the world's most famous footballer and held out my hand. '*Mr* Gascoigne, it's very nice to meet you.' Gazza shook hands with me and said 'Oh yeah, 'ow yer do' looking a little worried that he did not recognise this obviously well-connected woman. I left it at that but I had redeemed myself slightly in the eyes of those who had just heard my excessive profanity. When I spoke with several of those who had been present seven years later, at Dominic's wedding, at least they all remembered having met me before.

To be fair to the executives who suffered at Wembley

twice over they did invite me to their box at Old Trafford as a goodbye gift when they heard I was leaving to pursue football full time. I thought I behaved myself, but I cannot be sure.

Wearing your love of football on your sleeve has its advantages. If anyone had a spare ticket, they would call me. If anyone was meeting up for a drink with someone vaguely connected to the game they would call me. If anyone had a chance to meet Eric Cantona, the rest of the United team and a host of the Premiership's most famous players, they would pass it over and give it to me.

I played football in the park with Digby. He was an advertising copywriter with a burning desire to be a book critic who took football very seriously. He played extremely well. He was of slight build but had pace and skill and vision. He readily admitted that the reason he was a Derby County supporter was because he was bullied at a school where Derby were the favoured club.

'They just put me on a mini-bus one day. I did not know where it was going but we ended up at the Baseball Ground, and I've supported them ever since.' Digby was very serious and in the six years I knew him he never made a flippant comment. He acted as if awe-struck when my name started appearing in newspapers and I thought he was being sarcastic. He earned at least treble what I did, even though I was an editor and by then writing in my spare time for various nationals. All in all I was not terribly friendly towards him. I did not understand him. Then, one afternoon, he phoned me at work and said his friend, a film director, had been asked to make a commercial for Sky Sports' coverage of the Premiership. His friend knew nothing about football and had asked Digby to assist him.

Digby had said he was not up to it but he knew someone perfect for the job. Me. This sounded ridiculous. Digby was a mine of information about football, excelled at football quizzes and would love chatting with the great and the good. Why had he not put himself forward? But I was not about to pass up the opportunity to mingle with the cream of English soccer.

I was picked up by one of the vans carrying the camera crew and their equipment at a roundabout in north London. When we stopped at a service station the director's assistant wandered around checking who was who on the staff list. I was down as 'Football Advisor'. I could not make up my mind whether to laugh it off or take it seriously. I was sure every single make-up artist, lighting technician and tape editor knew as much about football as I did. I felt a bit of a fraud. Little did I know just how much hard labour lay ahead, how much essential knowledge I actually possessed.

The advert was being filmed at a smart five-star country hotel in Cheshire. A crew meeting was scheduled for 4 p.m. and with an hour to kill, I unpacked the football boots I had brought along just in case the pros fancied a five-a-side and were a player short or if the producer needed me to lay off balls to players as they lined up to shoot for the camera, and then I skulked around trying not to feel self-conscious. At the meeting pretty men in polo neck sweaters and girls in tight-fitting shimmering shirts and expensive lipstick managed to look involved and important. I sat down feeling frumpy and vague while the director, Lewis, explained just how much work we would all have to put in on Sunday and which scenes would be filmed inside and which outside. Lewis was a walking cliché of film luvviedom. He was delicate and fraught and at constant pains to emphasise that too much was being expected of him.

'And Alyson, make sure you are available at all times.'

Of course, but to do what exactly?

Scene One. This was in the hotel's leisure area. Lewis wanted a shot of the players in the Jacuzzi. 'Alyson, love, make sure the players are relaxed. Talk to them. Find out which ones are going to cause me problems. Find ways to make them animated.' I gulped, quietly. I had never met any of them before. What was I supposed to do, wander up to six famous men all in their swimming shorts and say hi, did you have a happy childhood?

There was nothing for it. I would have to employ my patented 'The way to talk to famous footballers' technique. So adopting a serious expression, I shook hands with them in turn. 'Hello, Mr Barmby, Mr Redknapp, how are you, I'm Alyson and it's my job to prepare you for filming. You know, make sure you're happy and know what to expect.' It worked a treat. We were on first name terms within seconds, of course. In fact it worked rather too well. A couple would not stand up without asking me about it first.

'Alyson, I don't want to talk to camera without you there.'

'It's all right, I'm going to be around all day.'

In the middle of the Jacuzzi session, Digby arrived. He sat huddled in a corner watching me ask the players about their favourite goals, their highlights of the previous season. Dalian Atkinson, then with Aston Villa, was proving particularly hard work. He would not smile or speak. He just shrugged and seemed generally displeased to be spending his Sunday with his feet dangling in an overcrowded bath tub. My job, it appeared, was to find a way to make him enthusiastic. I remembered he had scored the *Match of the Day* goal of the season and that after he had scored he had held his hands out in a 'What can I say, I can't help being so damn brilliant' sort of way. I asked him to recreate the scene and although he did not know why he had chosen that kind of celebration, he did at least smile at the memory.

When the Jacuzzi scene was over I thanked Digby for recommending me and asked why, if he was prepared to travel to Cheshire anyway, he had not said he would be Lewis' football advisor. 'I couldn't have done what you're doing. You're brilliant. I didn't know about Atkinson's goal. That was genius.' It was well-timed praise. It was only 10 a.m. and I was exhausted. Small talk and footballers is not a piece of cake.

Paul Ince arrived too late to experience any of this early 'soccer crèche with Alyson Rudd'. I spotted him in the bar as Lewis hissed in my ear that I had to talk to him before filming started.

This looked an even more difficult assignment. He was talking to his fellow footballers. I could not just barge in and interrupt. They were on a break from the day's work. I represented that work and would be out of line to set them all worrying about it again. I bided my time, hoping Mr Ince would need to leave the bar. He did and before I could jump in, he jumped in. 'Excuse me, do you play for Leyton Orient Ladies?' For years silly little girls must have run up to Paul Ince and asked, 'Excuse me do you play for West Ham/ Man United?' and here he was turning the experience on its head. Paul Ince pretended to recognise me before I spoke to him – I was very happy. 'Because I'm a big Orient fan,' he continued. For a split second I thought Ince might have actually seen me play, that he often wandered to our pitches near the reservoir and killed time leaning against his push-bike, pouring a cup of coffee from his thermos flask, quietly appreciative of the tackle that number 10 with the blonde hair had just made. Then it dawned on me that he must have asked who on earth that woman was who kept peering anxiously through the glass partition at him, and that the other footballers had said I was involved in the filming and had bored them to death trying to put my football life on a par with theirs.

Sadly, their assessment would have been correct. I had merrily swapped injury stories, goalscoring exploits stories and seen initial enthusiasm on their part turn to bewilderment that they, renowned professionals, were actually doing this. They were treating me as an equal and for a few minutes a genuine shared love of the game enabled them to forget they were talking to a girl. Mr Ince fortunately turned out to be helpful and fun and not in the least bit superior. He was indiscreet and gossipy but engagingly nervous in front of camera and remains to this day one of the nicest players I have ever met.

Scene Two was on the hotel's gravel driveway. In what to me seemed a stupid scenario, the players, all from different clubs, were to be glimpsed jumping out of Jeeps and Jags as if they were part of a Monkees film. Lewis wanted me in the scene. I did not have the nerve to tell him I suffered from motion sickness and all that stop start, in and out would result in me throwing up over Gary Speed's trousers, but the manner in which he abruptly gave up filming while darting a livid glare in my direction implies my green complexion did nothing to enhance that feeling of glamour he was trying to impart.

Scene Three was the Locker Room. I have given birth, I have broken my arm and my leg, but nothing, nothing compares to this. We used a very small changing room. At one end sat the footballers, at the other were the crew, the lighting and sound equipment, the director, and me. There was just enough space for everything but me, and I spent the next four hours crouching, stooping and bending as I cajoled performances out of the camera-shy players and all the while the heat from the lamps burned into my back. It was worth it, of course. I heard one player tell the director, as I tried to slip off for a breather that he would not say a single word unless I was the one asking the questions.

It was a bizarre session. I was inches from their faces, smiling, encouraging. There was no script so I guessed at what Sky might want them to say. Eventually a Sky executive muttered something to Lewis and he snapped that I was not getting them to say the right things. It was ridiculous. Chris Waddle was a natural and his first take was perfect, others were hopeless. Paul Ince got the giggles. 'Every time I look at you I just start laughing,' he said. And who could blame him? I had scraped back my enormous mop of hair and was as pink as a suckling pig on a spit. I did not care what I looked like. This had become another *Mission Impossible* and I wanted to prove I could accomplish it.

And then in strolled Eric Cantona, the most elusive, feted and sexy footballer in the country. My mind drifted back to the finishing school I never went to. 'So, young ladies, let's discuss appearances when meeting the rich and famous. Alyson, chiffon or fur?' 'Oh, probably a stained T-shirt, no make-up and lots of perspiration, Madame.'

Lewis brought me back down to earth. 'Which one is

this?' He pretended he had heard of Cantona. And tired of
how long each filmed interview was taking, Lewis brushed
me aside and said to Cantona: 'Can you say the Premiership
is bellissimo please, with lots of feeling.'

Cantona did not even raise an eyebrow. However, as
football advisor, I felt it my duty to take Lewis to one side
and tell him that Cantona was French, not Italian. 'OK, OK,
you take over then,' said Lewis sullenly with not a scrap of
gratitude. I spoke in French. 'Ah, you speak French?' asked
Cantona, his eyes sparkling just for a second at the thought
that the tedious afternoon would be made less tedious by
not having to struggle along in a language he clearly did
not have much affinity for. As soon as I said 'un peu', the
stock English answer when 'not really, I was just trying to
impress you' would be more accurate but, obviously, I did
not know how to say that in French, Cantona nodded and
shrugged.

He gave me his watch to hold as for him to have worn
it would have been inconsistent with the setting of a club
changing room at half time. 'Ah, un cadeau!' I joked. 'No,
I'll buy you one later,' he said. The executive and Lewis
both hissed through their teeth. 'Every second costs us
money, Alyson.' How on earth are real movies ever made
I thought. This was just a 40-second commercial, filmed in
one day, yet the director was on the verge of histrionics.

Scene Four was inside a squash court. Lewis wanted the
entire Manchester United team in a human pyramid with
the Premiership trophy at the top. I was not needed for
this and was made to feel my continued presence would
be a liability. Suddenly I was as expendable as the squash
court member who wanted to know why he could not play
a game at his usual hour. He wandered around with his

racquet looking very cross. Clearly he was not a United supporter. The children who had been told they could not swim while the players were by the pool were chuffed to bits their fun was being halted by their heroes.

It had been a tough weekend but as I dragged myself to the office on Monday morning I perked up. But for me Eric Cantona would have been portrayed as an Italian. I mentioned this to everyone who'd listen and many who wouldn't, at least not for a third time, but I was indulged and humoured, for I had returned bearing autographed goodies including a signed baby-sized Man United shirt for Ed's new son. Big, tough Mark Hughes had held the shirt up and said 'Ahh, isn't it tiny. Isn't it amazing what you can buy now?' before signing it, nodding knowingly when I said the baby's name was George.

Footballers are notoriously hard work. They have earned an obscene amount of money too young to understand its worth and been so mollycoddled by their clubs that they have few opinions worthy of debate. But during that weekend in Cheshire it was the players I felt most comfortable with. We had a common thread of experience which triumphed in spite of all the difficulties, my gender, my journalistic forcefulness, my lack of a generous cleavage, so that what could have been a belittling and unproductive weekend was really rather fun. The advertising and film staff were far less accommodating. Even those who were outwardly friendly maintained an air of aloofness. 'We're in TV,' they seemed to be saying. 'We dress and talk and smoke like TV people. You are not one of us, in fact you are close to being a freak.'

When at college I had on occasion mixed with the Toff set. This had been a fair trade because I mingled with them in order to have a laugh at their expense, and they had done likewise. But where I was prepared to say 'hi' on the Monday after the weekend dinner party as I passed Daphne in her candy striped shirt on her way to her tutorial, the Toff was not. There is a strong herd mentality to any group whether it be of media types or Toffs and they do not want to let you snuggle in too close.

The next day there were photographs in the papers of the players in the Jacuzzi printed in the national press. I cut one out and pinned it on the wall next to my desk before typing out an invoice for my weekend's work. Sky's response was that the job had been contracted out to Lewis and he was responsible for paying all members of the crew. Lewis, however, claimed he was over-budget and Digby asked me not to rock the boat. What price an Italian Cantona, a sour-faced Atkinson and a nervous Redknapp? Not a bean. Football advisors, who needs them?

CHAPTER EIGHTEEN

playing for two

He was young and keen, busy but not irritable. 'So, I expect you have a few questions,' he said with the air of one who is ready for anything and most of it will be routine, the stuff of old wives' tales.

'Can I carry on playing football?'

For a second he was lost for words, he opened his mouth but nothing came out, but it was only for a second. He recovered his composure with alacrity and feigned dismissiveness.

'Of course you can. We do not advocate taking up a brand new sport at this juncture but if your body is used to football then you can carry on playing it for as long as you feel comfortable.'

I was truly amazed. This was tremendous news. On learning I was pregnant I had assumed, with some ill-humour, that at least a year of not being allowed to play soccer lay ahead of me. 'I can see how I could play this afternoon,' I said 'but when should I stop, surely there is a point at which you have to stop.'

'No, that's entirely up to you,' and the obstetrician made a pleased-with-himself smacking noise with his lips and left.

It was then I drew up my grand plan. I would play

football until what? A month before delivery? That seemed reasonable in light of what I had just been told, and then I would re-start two days after giving birth. That way I would lose no more precious football time than if I had suffered a simple hamstring injury. I recalled that the marathon runner Liz McColgan had started training the day after having her first child and had given an interview in which she said that the strenuous nature of first carrying a child and then of childbirth had served only to increase her fitness levels. Ha, I would emerge from my chrysalis of confinement a new and improved athlete.

And for the next three weeks I zipped around Astroturf, real turf and concrete with renewed zeal. I had unbounded energy, team-mates commented on how fired up I was. After one game for Leyton Orient Ladies in which I played on the left wing, they could not praise me highly enough. They had learned by this point in my footballing career not to lavish compliments upon me, perceiving me to have little need of an ego boost, but they simply could not help themselves.

'Wow, Ally, I've never seen you work so hard, the way you beat their full-back to put in that cross was amazing, she had ten yards on you at least.' When I scored, having set up three goals for others the cheers were heartfelt. 'Hey, I'm glad you scored one, you deserved it,' commented one of my least favourite team-mates.

It was not just relief that I could participate that spurred me on, the hormones buzzing away inside my body had altered my physique, my use of oxygen was more efficient. I felt like the bionic woman, which was appropriate because I am a dead ringer for the young Lindsay Wagner. I laughed a lot during matches because I had a secret weapon. Was I the first pregnant footballer I wondered.

Then it started to go wrong. Like Jeff Goldblum in *The Fly*, my sudden and welcome surge of strength and energy was developing nasty side effects. I felt drained after games and full of guilt. My tummy ached and I started supping orange juice instead of beer afterwards. The defining moment came in a women's match. The ball was wellied clear by a stocky defender who did not care that I was three feet in front of her. The ball blasted into my stomach. I could almost hear the foetus crying 'Ouch. Enough, woman, for God's sake wake up to your responsibilities,' and I played timidly for the rest of the game convinced I was about to have a very public miscarriage.

Still, I clung to the obstetrician's advice. I carried on playing but I lost all that I had gained and more. I tiptoed through matches and pulled out of tackles. A group of men I knew solely because we played the addictive and far too time-consuming – 'I'm not paying £7 million for that duffer Stan Collymore' – 'fantasy football' together, were invited to play in a five-a-side tournament. They had never seen me play, only heard my boasts of incredible talent and inevitably I let them and myself down with a sluggish and sheepish display. I could not tell my secret, it would be grossly unfair to play with men or women while they knew of my predicament. 'Don't worry, if you mistime your challenge you could kill a child, that's all,' did not seem a fair proposition.

So I was forced to stop, a full five months earlier than I had planned. I was denied the opportunity to score a delicious side-foot volleyed goal only to go immediately into labour in my football kit. Had I really believed it was possible, that I could run around a field with two and a half extra stones of weight, a bulbous stomach and an indignant pelvic floor muscle? I had, simply because I knew so little of what pregnancy involved. My motto is that if you want it badly you can have it, and that damned obstetrician had led me to believe that I could. So, instead of 40 press-ups on a Tuesday evening I went to ante-natal classes where you squeezed your pelvic floor muscles 40 times instead.

The only class with a space left in it anywhere near my home was in Sloane Square. I probably need say no more. It was brimming with women who embraced their pregnancy as if it was all they had been put on this earth to do. Only one other girl admitted she had conceived accidentally but she vanished very quickly as if shamed by the wholesomeness of the sessions. I became conscious of the fact I was considered different. It was not just my northern accent, heck, I am considered posh by my football girls, it was everything.

'Close your eyes and let a soothing colour wash over you,' instructed the pregnancy advisor. I closed my eyes and saw the green and red of Anfield lit by warm sunshine. It was very soothing but apparently not what she had in mind. We were asked what our colour was and what it symbolised. Pink, said one expectant mum, because that was the colour of the nursery. Lavender, said another simply because it was her favourite shade. Orange was greeted with giggles, a little risqué, presumably, but the response 'Red and green' just drew a frown. I did not explain further. Sloane Rangers would assume Anfield must be the name of my grandmother's estate. I escaped that group, infiltrated another via the breast feeding propaganda class, and pretended I was a cookery writer for *Harpers & Queen* but it did not work. I was greeted with puzzlement even when I never mentioned football. But then I have learned that even when I think I have never mentioned something I usually have.

Never mind I thought, at least my birth will be easy because I am an athlete. Of course it wasn't and I presume there is some law or conspiracy which prevents graphic, accurate details of what childbirth is actually like, I won't attempt one here. It would be odd, would it not, for a football book to be banned because of obscene references to the cervix.

But at least the child was out. Time to get back to playing footie. We, the new mothers looking pained and in ghastly slippers, were shepherded into a room to be lectured on post-natal health and fitness.

'So, I expect you have a few questions,' said the nurse.

'When can I,' I hesitated, there was an entire room of women just waiting to be alienated but then I thought, I don't want to risk being given the wrong advice because I skirted around the subject. 'When can I start playing football again?'

'Football? Mmm. Several months.'

'Months? But Liz McColgan . . .'

The nurse clicked her teeth in exasperation. 'That Liz McColgan has a lot to answer for.' And she proceeded to explain that while some women might feel able to take up strenuous exercise immediately after giving birth any that did would be hospitalised 20 years later by acute incontinence. Yuk. I suppose I should have been grateful that my midwife was not, well, Liz McColgan, and I had been saved an embarrassing and uncomfortable middle age, but I was distraught. I had vowed, laid money on the fact I would be back in the park within two weeks of releasing baby. Watching me glower, the nurse laughed and said 'Anyway, you'd look a sight wouldn't you running around a football pitch with your inflated breasts leaking milk.' As

I hobbled back to my ward I wondered if I would ever, ever play again. Mother nature hates women footballers, I thought.

I embarked upon motherhood without the network of cooing emotionally disturbed sisterhood granted to everyone else. At the doctor's surgery, while waiting for my baby to be weighed, I struck up a conversation with a stranger, a woman with an incredibly small daughter. She asked what I did for a living and it all came out; football this football that and she sighed and said 'It's lucky you had a boy then.' She was right. It would not be fair to sentence any daughter to the fate, the degree of ostracism, I had suffered. My son was kicking a ball at nine months old and being instructed to use both feet at two. All that 'they learn in the womb' stuff must be true.

Football had not been an uninterrupted stream of happiness prior to falling pregnant, however. Only three summers into obsession I had broken my wrist. I did not realise this at the time. I had been tackled and fallen onto dusty, hard ground that had seen no grass for months and gradually felt my arm stiffen. In complete innocence, and only because my team-mates had advised me to, I skipped into the Accident and Emergency department. I gave my name and address to the receptionist and then turned to face the waiting room. It was jam-packed with miserable faces, everyone muttering about how long they had been stuck there. 'There's a four-hour wait, by the way,' added the receptionist. I spied a chair and clambered over several old men and a young lad holding a bloody bandage to sit next to a middle-aged woman. She wiped away a tear.

'What have you done, dear?' she asked.

'Just hurt my arm, that's all. And you?'

She blew into her hankie. 'I've got the most terrible pain in my head. I went to my GP and he thinks it could be a blood clot but I've been sat here for three hours. I could drop dead for all they care.' So we sat in awkward silence for 15 minutes and then my name was called. As I stood up, the clot woman bristled. 'This is ridiculous,' she hissed as I walked up to the nurse. She held my wrist in her hand and, with the authority of someone who knows everything and does not see the need for X-rays or doctors or specialists, she said, 'That's broken. And so you can jump the queue. This way.'

As I followed her I tried to correct her. 'I don't think it is broken. I hardly felt a thing, I shouldn't be wasting your time really.' But hospitals love patients who under-estimate their injuries and I was led past a line of people, all waiting to be X-rayed, and presumably insisting that they should be, to receive immediate attention. As I sat waiting to see the doctor who would remark upon the X-ray, I felt tears pricking at my eyes. What a sight I was, a grown woman sat in a football shirt and track-suit bottoms, her chin quivering because she faced the prospect of being denied a kick-about in the park. But at that moment I felt truly tragic.

'So how did we do this then?' asked the doctor.

'I was tackled playing football and I fell onto my wrist.'

'Excellent.'

'Sorry?' I had anticipated a lecture on how NHS funding was not supposed to be swallowed up by sports injuries but this doctor was delighted to be treating me.

'Far better to be hurt while doing something that is healthy for you. I see so many people hurt because they fall off their chair or slip on the ice outside their front door. We'll have you plastered and better in no time so you can get back to playing.' I cheered up the way the child cheers up after screaming because it has to have an inoculation but is offered a lollipop out of a big jar by a kindly matron.

I trudged off home wearing a sling, went to bed and woke up the next morning confronted by the complex puzzle of how to wash and dress with one hand. My cat wanted to know how I was going to open his tin of food. I phoned my office to explain why I was late.

'You've got to come in, Alyson,' said Angus, the keen, nervy junior reporter.

'Why? There's nothing happening today anyway.'

Angus sighed anxiously. 'There's a reason,' he said at last.

'What reason? Don't be silly.'

'There's something here for you that you have to deal with today.' I tried to remember if we had published anything controversial. 'Is it a writ?' 'No, but sort of – you have to come in.'

I got there at 4 p.m. Angus beamed and led me into the basement where a bouquet of flowers had been put in a bucket. 'We thought we'd keep them in here as it's cool,' he said proudly. Then, noticing that I had not fallen into a swoon and whispered 'Oh, pink chrysanthemums, my favourite,' Angus started to blink rapidly. 'I thought you'd want them for the weekend. I mean someone's gone to the trouble of sending you flowers, I didn't think you'd want them to go to waste.'

'Angus,' I said, 'How am I going to *get* them home for the weekend. I've only got one hand, I kind of need that for hauling myself onto the bus.'

There was a card. The flowers were from John, the super-fit 45-year-old who had made the tackle, and Pete, the player who had invited John to play. It was all so ridiculous. It turned out that Angus had assured them I would come in to the office and so it was safe to send the flowers there. I phoned Pete, partly to thank him and partly to complain that he would not have sent a bouquet to Tom or Digby or Dave if they had broken their arm, so why undermine me with sexist nonsense. But Pete anticipated my reaction.

'Now don't get huffy about it, Ally. We're very fond of you and thought you might need cheering up, that's all. And if you were a bloke you wouldn't have fallen so pathetically.' So I stuffed the flowers in the gap between my sling and my chest and tried to walk tall as I ventured back home. Secretly I was pleased to be sent flowers, no one ever sends tough-as-old-boots Alyson anything remotely feminine. It was ironic it had taken football to bring out my muliebrity.

It happened again 18 months later. We were on our six-a-side pitch and a player short. A straggler had asked for a game and we let him join in. He was the sort, though, that wanders around sports complexes trying to make an impression. He was too big and too fierce for our game, and he took it far too seriously. During my spell in goal, he was unmarked, with the ball, and ready to shoot. There was no need for him to hit the ball as hard as he did and if I had thought about it I would not have tried to save it. But I did. 'Hey, great save, Ally,' came the shout as I felt my wrist crumple and turn to jelly. 'Someone else's turn then,' I said. This time I knew it was broken and was so pre-occupied with that thought that I dribbled past two challenges, placed a lovely shot beyond the keeper and opened the gate. The team looked puzzled. 'Just off to casualty,' I shouted.

My other problem was my knees. In the early days they never ached when I played but they, and in particular the left one, felt sore and creaky if I went clubbing or sometimes even if I just walked down the street. I bypassed the GP. What I needed was someone who took football seriously. Pete asked around for me and came up with the BIMAL clinic in west London. This was where Princess Di and Will Carling were eventually caught out but it had not achieved such notoriety when I first attended. No, what impressed me was my physio's ability to drop hundreds of famous footballing names into the conversation. It was *the* place for sore knees.

There were plenty of gadgets to keep my ingenuousness steaming along nicely. One machine measured leg muscle strength. I had to press against a padded bar while sitting down which I did rather feebly until the physio injected a note of competition into the exercise. He could compare my efforts with those of top sportsmen and women. My left leg was fairly ordinary, the weak side of average, but my right was the strongest female leg on their books (per body weight). This was not exactly helping my knee but the whole 'we'll treat you like a pro' approach had me hooked. And, after a couple more sessions, my knee felt great. I was sorry to have to leave. I could get very used to being regularly told my right leg breaks the record books. The best piece of advice my physio offered me was to drive an automatic. It was the clutch work which was potentially ruining my football career.

Five years later I was running down the wing to catch up with a hopelessly over-hit pass when I felt my right knee buckle. I tried to ignore it but something was clearly wrong so I lay behind the goal and stared at the knee. It looked all right. But then when I tried to bend it, it locked. Panic stricken I rested it again for a couple of minutes and it was fine. I jumped up, strolled about and looked over at the game I had just left. It was one of our better matches. Eight-a-side on a balmy evening. I could not resist rejoining it. I'll just not kick the ball, I thought. This was, I know, akin to going for a dip in the sea while trying to swim around the salt, or eating a fry-up without the cholesterol, but the drug of football just pulled me back in. The ball bounded in my direction. It was not quite at head height but I stooped anyway and made a pretty decent effort of it.

'Good header, Ally.'

This is working out fine, I thought. Then the ball was passed to me along the ground. A voice somewhere in my head told me to ignore it, to walk off the pitch, to put long-term health before immediate gratification. I tried a first time cross. A sharp pain shot through my knee and I collapsed in a heap. My knee had popped out of its socket.

By this time BIMAL was far too famous and full. I was offered an appointment at some date inside the next millennium. They had no record of my previous consultations and I think doubted their existence. My protestations that my footballing career was under threat impressed no one. I sought out a local physio. I cross-examined her heavily as to her familiarity with sports injuries before agreeing to an examination, but my physio was not only competent but sincere. My bleatings about how imperative it was that I be back on a football field immediately were not greeted with an arched eyebrow or puckered lips, and she even offered to tape my knees into place the day before each game to ensure that while I worked on rectifying my problem, I had a knee that did not ping. The idea is that the tape is just taut enough 24 hours after application. Immediately after being put on it is so tight that I would walk from the clinic to home as if I had just attended a John Wayne convention.

I hoped the acres of dark, heavy duty tape across my knees would make me look tough and menacing. My team in the park were either amused or concerned that I should be playing at all. The tape would not stay on for a complete game and players would intermittently stop and stare at the ground then gingerly pick up pieces of my leg dressing and hand them to me as if they were as important as some false teeth or as disgusting as a Tampax. I have noted, since, that men, whether in the park or in the Premiership, do not trot out for games with their knee caps Sellotaped into position. This is because, from what I can discern about my disability, the problem is one of under-developed, essentially girlie, muscle, being pulled about by over-developed, not normal for a girlie, muscle. And because I only play football and rarely swim or jog or pull on a lycra body-suit to dance aerobically, how else?, to Bryan Adams, the same old muscles are neglected and the others promoted.

Many of us in the park are starting to creak and wobble. Tom has pins in his shoulders and plays as though he is carrying a tray of aperitifs. Orrin is younger than many but came off the worst in a collision with a road sweeper and drifts between being at 80 per cent and 90 per cent of his former fearless self. Ray insists on playing in another game immediately prior to ours so that he is infuriatingly breathless and unable to chase the slightest of over-hit passes. Sean and Conor complain that their eye-sight is failing. Adrian has pieces of calcified bone floating around his ankles. Mick stops for a drink before we play and his consequent late tackles make life doubly difficult for Tom, Orrin, Ray, Sean, Conor, Adrian and everyone else who feels it is their turn to moan about their aches and pains. When I have been forced to be a mere spectator of our matches I am staggered that the combative yet skilful contests I feel them to be while taking part are in fact painfully slow, as if we are a hospital patients' side playing to aid recuperation. Or if Mick has supped too enthusiastically, the team appears to be in a scene from *One Flew Over the Cuckoo's Nest*, all of them being indulged in the fantasy that they are playing soccer when in fact they are actually running around a car park head-butting each other.

Some men buy toupées, others conduct affairs with women half their age, but park footballers fend off the advancing years by kicking a ball even when it hurts to do so. And for myself, I intend to play on and on, regardless of my pop tart knees, of how ludicrous I may look, and how mortified my son will one day be.

CHAPTER NINETEEN

extra time

Time to go to the children's playground. It was a mild, still and colourless March afternoon. I trundled the push chair along the path that leads to the slides but Sam, my two-year-old son, sprang out of the buggy and stood and watched some primary school children playing a game of football. He wanted to join in. I told him he was too small but if he stood next to me, maybe when the ball was kicked out of play he could kick it back to them. The ball never quite reached him. He stared at it intently, mesmerised, occasionally turning to look up at me to say, 'I want to play *foot*ball.'

The game ended and the children fooled about while they gathered their coats together. I told Sam he could play with their ball for a short while and I shouted to the eight-year-olds. 'He wants to join in, will you let him kick your ball for a bit.' They passed the ball to Sam and laughed as he ever so seriously passed it back. 'Hey, he's good. How old is he?' one boy said. Soon they had gone and Sam was sad. Then he spotted two slightly older boys passing the ball in a triangle with what looked like their older sister. Sam ran up to them and one of the boys knocked the ball toward him, his return pass was swift and accurate and the boys squealed in delight. The girl automatically deferred to Sam and drifted away from the triangle, even a two-year-old male has his place in the soccer hierarchy. The triangle became two nine-year-olds and my toddler. Then they started running with the ball and tackling each other. Sam ran and tackled too. 'He's going to be a brilliant player,' called one of the boys.

I felt very proud. Very, very proud. I was out of plaster but my left foot was still sore after the break and it crossed my mind that this was how it would be now. I would live my football life through my son. He would play in the first team, win trophies and eventually play for his country. My eyes moistened.

The next day I visited my physio. On the previous visit she had asked me to jump on my sore foot and I had been unable to do so. Playing again had seemed so far away. But I had religiously stuck to her exercise plan and this time I could jump with ease and I Zebedee'd across the hospital floor. She told me to put my trainers on and we went outside. 'Jog,' she ordered, so I jogged. 'Faster,' she said. 'So when can I play football?' I asked. 'Three, maybe four weeks,' she answered. Poor Sam, one day he will have to tell his friends the reason his mum is not watching him playing is because she is. Perhaps he will lie.

I immediately set about regaining my fitness and jogged to the nearby cricket field. I sprinted and then jogged again. When I returned home I felt sick and continued to feel sick for two days. I had overdone it. I had limped from sofa to chair to car and back again for two months. My heart had been in permanent snooze mode and I had woken it too suddenly. My stupidity delayed my return to the beautiful game by seven days.

At last I was ready. I laid my Liverpool shirt out on the bed at one o'clock, five hours before kick-off. I made a special trip to the supermarket for an isotonic sports drink. 'I'll need an isotonic drink especially today,' I thought, even though I know full well isotonic just means drinkable.

And so Year Ten began. I arrived at Regent's Park three minutes early. The rain was gentle but incessant. I passed three tourists dressed in smart cream raincoats, their arms linked as they walked past the fountains and the perfect flower beds. I turned the corner expecting to see my team-mates huddled under a tree, changing into their kit, but there was no one there. The entire patch of park that on sunnier days holds a hundred or more players was deserted. I stood still and gawped. There was only one thing to do and that was go for a walk. While I was gone everyone would arrive. I just was not in the mood for one of those evenings where I stand and wait and watch each member of my team walk agonisingly slowly towards me with three- to seven-minute gaps between each arrival.

Fifteen minutes later I returned and a game was underway. I did not recognise any of the players but never mind I thought, I will be brave and ask them if I could join in. But Lionel had thought of that first and was already playing with them. I had not recognised him because he was wearing a sweatshirt over his trademark Arsenal shirt and he was ill, the Gunners having had a bumper Easter that deserved perpetual boozing.

In the end only seven of my park regulars showed. Gary and I stood next to each other as we changed. Everyone has a chance to claim they changed next to Gary because he takes so long to put his kit on. I had brought my boots with the extra long studs. It had rained non stop for a fortnight and even Regent's Park would be squelching I had thought. I pulled one of the boots out of its carrier bag. Gary stared. He stared the way actors in horror films stare when an act of unbelievable grossness is unfolding before their eyes. These particular boots had seen no daylight for at least 18 months. The mud on them had set rock hard and the moisture trapped inside had shrunk the shoe. I struggled to fit my foot inside giving a passable rendition of an ugly sister with a glass slipper. 'Ugh, arrgh, it's so uncomfortable, I'm not sure I can keep it on.'

'When did you last clean your boots Ally?' asked Gary. He was offering me an opening, a chance to redeem myself. He wanted to hear me say I had forgotten to clean them the last time I used them and then forgotten that I had forgotten. But I can be cruel. 'I never clean my boots,' I replied. 'Life's too short.' Gary, the obsessive-compulsive, gulped. He looked down at his own boots as the rain slipped gracefully off their sheen. 'I clean mine every week, *without fail*,' he said, less with pride than with defiance. Here he was right and I was wrong. Gary played a blinder in his studs and I, having been forced back into my Astroturf boots, slipped at every turn.

The other team, the team we had never seen before, had only nine players so they were happy to join forces. We played each other and took a ten-year-old from their team to even up the numbers. I seriously began to think I had strolled through a Wormhole in space-time on my second journey past the flower beds. This other team, they had corresponding players. They had our names. There was even an Ally, short for Alistair. And at the end their captain said, 'We're here every Thursday evening, so if you want to join in just let us know.' No, I thought, no, you're not.

We are here every Thursday evening and have been for the past one hundred summers. How dare you treat us as novices. Why, I have never even seen any of you before. My team-mates were all thinking the same thing but Gary said, 'Thursdays, right, thanks guys.'

There was a reason they adopted possession of the park, why they felt within their rights to issue us with an invitation to our own party. We had played so, so badly. Ben was heavily hung-over, Frank was not there, Ricky played as though he had talent and indulged in turns and flicks that he was not up to and even when they came off he was so surprised he failed to follow them through. Gary, as usual, played well but could not be everywhere at once and I looked retarded.

I made the big mistake of warning their captain that this was my first game back from injury. Every time I touched the ball thereafter he would turn to me and say 'You all right?' Hardly. I had no pace, and when I kicked the ball it trickled when I had been aiming for a long range chip and it whooshed when I had been trying a gentle lay-off. I was giving a pretty darn good impression of a woman who had never played football before. My back heel to Lionel, a shot on the turn and a volley from a corner only served to turn that impersonation into one of a woman who has never played football before who is lucky.

We were so out of it that eventually one their players swapped sides in place of the boy. The boy had been old enough to know what to do yet chose to sulk standing in front of our keeper. If the ball happened to roll near him he would lift his foot up and let it pass by. Not, I would venture, a boy destined to grow up to be a highly sought-after professional. Unlike my toddler. Sam would have been more use to us. Not that I am planning on bringing him along so that new players can say, 'What's that bloody woman doing on the pitch with her sodding baby.' Once we had one of their players we played well. He took charge, scored a goal, set a few up and the game was transformed. What a fillip to his self-esteem it must have been and when I told him so he laughed and said, 'Yeah, I'm Dennis Bergkamp really.'

Still, it was good to be back. Ricky still has no idea who most of us are, and he is from the Year Five intake. We have three members called Dave, one of whom had promised to attend but did not. 'So, which Dave is that?' asked Ricky, 'Is he the one with dodgy ankles?'

'We've all got dodgy ankles, Ricky, it's the Dave with the dodgy back.'

'I thought Tom had the dodgy back.'

'He has, but his shoulder is worse than his back so we don't call him dodgy back Tom.'

We are a bunch of geriatrics, small wonder we were thrashed. The other team were younger, fitter and more talented. What hope did we have?

Prior to the next match in the park my Sam tried to join in a game being played with seven-year-olds. They were just young enough to be without magnanimity and instead of passing to the toddler, they delighted in flicking the ball past him. 'Mummy,' he screamed, 'they're not sharing.' But I did not intervene. Life is full of hard lessons even when you are two. And so, aware that his mother was not about to help out, little Sam stopped chasing the ball and began chasing the boys instead. He growled at them like a Rottweiler puppy and banged his fists against their knees. They fell to the ground in mock submission and then allowed him to kick their ball. That's my boy.

My second game back after injury was not much better. I spent three hours finding the bits and pieces of my kit, which included one hour emptying the airing cupboard searching for socks that had lain crumpled, unwashed in a carrier bag under the stairs the whole time. Only Patrice was in the park when I arrived. Patrice is of the Year Eight intake and was tiring of being asked for World Cup tickets just because he is French. Even if he had asked for tickets the authorities would not have believed him, his accent is straight from *Allo Allo*. His shrugs, his eyebrow movements as he strolls around the pitch are a pastiche of Cantona. The first time I met him I thought he was acting. But no, he is, simply, French.

In the end we were forced into joining forces once again. It was a different team, a more frivolous team whose players all thought they were Norman Wisdom and kept falling over on purpose before tripping up someone else. It was an annoying match. Every ten minutes one of their players would leave and another of ours would turn up. Then the new arrivals dried up and the game slowly shrank and we kept swapping players over to even up the numbers. Suddenly it was four against three and all over. I never felt the game had really begun. I was bad, again. But that was not simply because I was still regaining my fitness and touch. It was a game in which no one passed the ball. It was all crosses and individualism. I received the ball wide on the right wing and paused. One of their players said, 'Watch her, watch her, she's better than she looks.' Someone sniggered. Christ, I thought, it is like starting all over again from the very beginning.

The following week was much better. We did not need to mix with outsiders and we played a spirited five-a-side. The wind buffeted us and the ball which swerved around in mid-air. I strained my neck to reach a cross but at the crucial moment the wind seized the ball and instead of planting a firm header I planted a firm nose. I scored, later, at least and felt a little quicker and fitter than I had the week before. Sean brought along his teenage nephew, who hid his astonishment at our geriatric gyrations very well. He floated past each challenge with the nonchalance of youth. 'You must play for Eire Under-18s or something,' I said to him, only half joking. 'No,' he replied, 'I don't play football at home at all.'

Still, we enjoyed ourselves. Lionel was in knit one purl one mode whereby a cross so inaccurate that we expected to hear glass breaking in the distance was followed by one so accurate it was embarrassing not to score from it with your eyes closed. I had shouted out that only tap-in goals would count, which was not meant to be taken literally, it was just a way to encourage the guys not to use the wind and score from goalkicks. But it meant that 20-yard drives would be greeted with shouts of 'What a lovely tap-in' and no one knew the valid score.

Next to our little passion play, another group was engaged in a five-a-side game. They had four women playing and they were not, as far as I was aware, squealing. 'That's nice' I thought. But something was wrong, something made the women look out of place. I could not immediately work out what it was so I stopped staring at them. Later, it hit me. The girls had been wearing tight leggings. No matter how well a woman might play, she will be undermined if she wears leggings instead of shorts or track-suit bottoms.

Really, football is everywhere, in every shop window, in every newspaper, on every TV show, but somehow some women fail to notice that footballers wear shorts and socks. That is surely not so difficult is it? Would they wear a bikini to a funeral or a waistcoat on the beach? No, they would probably wear those silly leggings.

Orrin opted to play for the talented team, the one with Dennis Bergkamp. He was rejecting us. This had never happened before. We were stunned but could not summon much sarcasm for we all understood. Orrin is too good for us, we cannot expect him always to play with the remedials. I watched him in the distance, and next to another bunch of players he looked different, less majestic, more serious.

It will take weeks if not months before I look the part once more and then the moments of beauty will be mere droplets against a puddle of dross. Those special seconds must be incredible for a gal to put up with all the paraphernalia of lost shin-pads, late arrivals and embarrassing shots off target. And they are. I don't know for sure that a baseball player feels differently about a big hit or how hockey players feel in their finest hour, but football has something. It has an endearing simplicity. You cannot use your arms so you jump and use your forehead, trap the ball on your chest, tease the ball with your toes, your heel, your instep, the outside of your boot. It is baseness transformed into elegance. When the ball dips right where you want it to, when you slide in and beat the keeper, your blood curdles and your brain empties. The body is ignored as the soul bursts free. There is no memory, no fear, no pain. Only an intense happiness, a happiness without complications. I love you he said, but why, do I love him; a thoughtful gift from a friend, but I didn't buy her one; I'm pregnant but will it have five toes on each foot; it is sunny, warm, the sea is clear but will someone steal my purse; a goal, I have scored a goal, no buts, no thoughts, just an undiluted indefinable blast of happiness.

On the radio a ballerina talks about leaving her vocation and becoming clinically depressed. 'It was a death,' she says. Life without football would be a death, too. I see myself at 60, hair pure white, still too long, my hips on the waiting list, my face and arms deeply creased. My knee-caps pop out every quarter of an hour but I have learned how to squeeze them back into place without fuss. My football shirt is an original, a quarter of a century old and half the team have barely heard of third division Liverpool. Then someone sneers and says, 'What's that bloody granny doing on the pitch?' And I smile as I slide in, steal the ball off him and potter down the pitch to score yet again.

More Sport from Headline

Sir Les
The Autobiography of
Les Ferdinand

'Refreshingly outspoken . . . One of the best footballer's
autobiographies in the long time' *Goal*

Les Ferdinand is not just an exceptionally talented
footballer, he is a level-headed, thoroughly nice bloke with
strong views who has become a role model to many. He has
always been prepared to speak out on issues such as racism
in soccer and, in this updated edition of his autobiography,
he talks openly about:

- His two seasons at Newcastle United, including the
sensational departure of Kevin Keegan and the arrival of
Kenny Dalglish

- The deal that took him to boyhood favourites Tottenham
Hotspur for a club record £6 million and his first season
with Spurs

- His on-off involvement in the England set-up under
Terry Venables and his part in Glenn Hoddle's 1998
World Cup campaign

Idolised wherever he has played, Les Ferdinand's story –
from his early days on a west London council estate,
through his formative years at Queens Park Rangers, to his
status as one of the country's brightest stars – is sure to be
an inspirational read for all his fans.

NON-FICTION / AUTOBIOGRAPHY / SPORT 0 7472 5749 3

More Sport from Headline

All Quiet on the Hooligan Front

COLIN WARD

Is football going through a golden age or have the post-Hillsborough changes diluted those things that made the game special? Colin Ward, author of the hugely successful *Steaming In*, assesses how the mood of English football has developed in recent years, and vividly shows how it is still possible for fans to have great fun following their team. While hooliganism may be on the decline, the advent of a changing atmosphere, including drugs and the corporate culture, has brought new problems to the football grounds. This is a brilliant book that reveals so much about the way of life of so many football fans.

'Funny and touching' *The Scotsman*

'This explosive, no-holds barred book . . . written by a man who cares passionately about the game he loves' *Irish Post*

'His observations will certainly strike a chord with many fans' *FourFourTwo*

'Undiluted fan-memoir, not the sweet Hornby kind but raw lager-chucking sectarianism' *Independent on Sunday*

NON-FICTION / SPORT 0 7472 5867 8

If you enjoyed this book here is a selection of other bestselling sports titles from Headline